# LIGHT AFTER DARKNESS
## — an experience of Nicaragua

## by BETTY PURCELL

GW00691955

'(Ben) had a dream, of a Nicaragua where the day would not end for people as soon as the sun went down. He wanted to provide light after darkness for Nicaraguans to read and talk by. For that he was killed.'

— Elizabeth Linder, speaking of her son Ben, who was killed with two Nicaraguan colleagues in a Contra attack, April 1987.

## Attic Press
## Dublin

First published in 1989 by
Attic Press,
44 East Essex Street,
Dublin 2.


Purcell, Betty
    Light after darkness: an experience of
    Nicaragua
    1. Nicaragua. Social conditions
    I. Title
    972.85′053

    ISBN 0-946211-76-0 Pbk


Cover Design: Paula Nolan.
Typesetting: Phototype-Set Ltd., Dublin.
Printing: Guernsey Press.
Cover photograph: Derek Spiers.
Nicaraguan photographs: Kate Hughes, Paul Laverty.

# Contents

# DEDICATION

To the people of Nicaragua

I want to thank Donal O'Kelly for being with me all the way from Heuston Station, and for his enthusiastic support and encouragement in writing this book. Also Paul Laverty, Kate Laverty and Kate Hughes, who convinced me it was important to try and write it down. For Pushpinder Khaneka and Maureen Meehan, for their friendship and for showing me what foreign news reporting should be. For Eadaoin Heussaff, who travelled with me in Nicaragua, and for her invaluable contribution in shaping the final product. For Sofia Montenegro, Maria Gomez and Elizabeth Linder for turning their personal suffering into a spirit that embodies Nicaragua. For their friendship, help and continuing interest in Nicaragua, Roisin Boyd, Derek Speirs, Mary Purcell, Anne Daly and Kintilla Heussaff. Also the publishers, Attic Press.

Finally, but certainly not least, I want to thank Katie for being so good in allowing me to write this book during her first year of life.

# Managua — The Legacy of an Earthquake

The heat is the first thing that hits you. Before I had cleared customs, I was soaking wet. The air was more uncomfortable than walking around in a sauna, because it was damp. It made you feel weak and bad-tempered in the same moment, and in desperate need of a drink. All the warnings about water and ice were forgotten as I gratefully bought a pink sugary mineral, and tried to throw it back. The first shortage hit me. Because of the lack of bottles, the mineral was poured into a plastic bag full of ice. Looking around I saw a woman bite the corner off the bag and suck out the juice. As I tried to do the same, more trickled down my face and t-shirt than anything else. I gulped down what I could, and resolved to learn the trick. As quickly as possible. In the meantime I was a sticky mess.

The first impression of Nicaragua is of poor clothes, much laughter (about what I can't catch) and a slow pace. It amazes me how quickly the lifestyle at home seems hysterical and nonsensical when you move away. You wonder whether all the dashing around is really necessary, or how much of it is a way of proving our importance to ourselves. Nicaraguans are not impressed by hurry; there's no point in the tropical heat. People's clothes are old, some darned and patched, all spotlessly clean. Children, mainly barefoot, dash around playing games despite the heat. Ten minutes after arriving I can feel a dusty grime settling into every pore of my hands and face. I'm in a hurry to get a wash and rest.

I'm approached by a taxi man who offers 'city centre'. Following him, I find his car is a 1950s Chevrolet complete with leather buttoned seats and room for a mobile bar in the back. Later I was to find out that there are two kinds of taxi in Managua. The first belong to the old taxi-men, who pre-date the Sandinista triumph. They operate mainly around the Hotel Intercontinental, still maintain their old but solid petrol-guzzling giant cars, and spend their time condemning the government. The second type of cab is a battered small car, usually Japanese and rusted, with the name of one of the city co-operatives emblazoned on the side. These taxis cost about half what the big ones charge. The taxi-men take bargaining in pidgin Spanish in good part, and will usually halve the price they first mentioned. With a laugh. But this wisdom comes later. For now I'm happy to pay anything to get to a welcoming house, and sleep.

Managua is a city without a centre. This is mainly due to the 1972 earthquake which destroyed the central shopping and housing area, and left heaps of rubble where people should be. Many people said to me that it was Somoza's misappropriation of international relief that sealed his fate seven years later. Managuans suffered so much; hardly a family was not touched in some way by the earthquake tragedy. A friend, Danilo, told me how his grandmother was killed and his family made homeless. He had been only eight, yet he remembered from that day that his mother cried a lot, something he had never seen her do before. With her own mother dead and the family living in a makeshift wooden shelter, he reckoned she had just given up. After a while, his father found a small house which he also used for his trade, television mending. The family's living room to this day is full to bursting with televisions in various states of repair. They have made a new life. But Danilo's mother never got over the effects of the earthquake. She herself died two years later.

Nicaragua's leaders at the time failed to pass on the international aid sent, or to begin to reconstruct the city. The only significant building to survive was the Hotel Intercontinental. The hotel, along with many of the middle and upper class houses of Bolonia, was built specifically to withstand tremors. These buildings remain in what is still the 'embassy belt' of Managua, surrounded on all sides by shanties and the small new houses of the poor.

Where is the centre of Managua? Everyone I asked seemed to have a different answer. The Plaza de la Revolucion, where big marches end. The ruins of the old Catholic cathedral, now sometimes used for films and cultural events. The Hotel Intercontinental, meeting-place for journalists and visitors. Plaza Espana, where Managua's most popular bakery stands. The train station, from where revamped trams trundle north and south. Centroamerica, or Plastic City, where the young find ice-cream, pizzas and discos.

When you give up looking for the 'centre', you start to ramble as the city rambles; it spreads out for miles of suburbs each with its own pivotal place. There are still rich and poor areas, mixed areas, the total poverty of newly-arrived refugees from the war zones, and the settled near-comfort of the older working class. The new system has not brought complete equality. It has started with providing the poorest with the basic social needs of housing, food and health, rather than seizing all the assets of the richest. Some observers have argued that the economic transformation has not gone deep enough. The Sandinistas' reply is that there is a price to be paid for attempting to bring along as many of the people as possible with you. That price is allowing some inequality still, but giving everyone the basics, and the promise of further change down the road. It's a risky business in a climate of scarcity. But people can see the effects of the first phase of redistribution. Everyone has a house to live in.

Because people's houses are small, a lot of activity takes place in the streets. Here the street vendors sell their dinners of pork and chicken, rice and beans. They are served on giant leaves from banana trees, the same leaves which are used to wrap eggs for transport. My first evening in Nicaragua was spent wandering 'downtown', or what seemed like the direction of town, from the quiet housing of middle-class Managua to the buzzing areas of working-class life, where children and pets thronged the streets, and adults enjoyed that most precious of human recreations, the chat. Not for the last time I was struck by this similarity to Irish people, particularly Irish country people. A real understanding of the importance of conversation exists, and most tasks are not so urgent that they won't hold until a story or argument is finished.

Passing by a government building of some kind, I'm struck by the demeanour of the soldiers protecting the building. Here they are, chatting and laughing, the teenagers flirting with one another and waving easily in my direction. This is amazing after experiencing other countries in the region, where a tough machismo dominates the army and police. I can see why many people thought in the early days that the naïveté of Nicaragua's new regime would make them easy to overcome militarily. Yet the truth is belied by the image. Over the next six months I was to learn how the Sandinistas could fight when they were put to it.

A woman friend who worked as a housekeeper in Managua was waiting excitedly for the return of her eldest son from the war front, where he had spent the previous two years. On his return, she introduced us. He was only nineteen, and a less tough person you couldn't imagine, yet he had been a member of one of the crack squads in the Nicaraguan army which pursues Contras into the jungle to take them on. Unusually for Latin America, he didn't seem to mind helping his mother wash the dishes while he talked about how good it was to be back in the comfort of home. There was very little meat to be had the whole period he was away, and he told me, without any sensationalism, how they used to catch monkeys to eat. These were more plentiful in the heart of the jungle than the iguanas (giant lizards) which were the other form of available meat. You made great friends in the army, he said, and risking your lives together created a special bond that would not ever disappear. But you also realised the value of home, of quiet, of reading and the friendship of women, all of which were absent at the front. The only question he didn't want to answer was how many Contras he had killed. It was clear from a certain sadness in his look that he had seen death at close hand, but he looked on it as necessary but tragic, not a subject for idle conversation. He was praying the war would end before his younger brother would have to go.

Walking down a side street on that first night I passed a substantial enough building, headquarters of the Conservative Party. Out the door and down the steps flowed gallons of water. This struck me as odd, because there was water rationing at the time. Later a friend told me that this was quite a regular occurrence. The Conservatives would leave their taps running at night, so the water gushed down the tile floors and steps and out into the street. They believed that civil and governmental annoyance at such waste of a scarce commodity would lead to their being repressed. Perhaps this analysis was a bit far-fetched, but I could find no other explanation for the overnight floodings. In any case nothing was ever done against the party for doing this, and eventually they gave it up.

Turning out of the side streets where most of the housing now stands, you find yourself on a wide avenue leading down from the Intercontinental on your right to the old Cathedral about a mile away. The avenue looks as though it was always wide and imposing, but the buildings which used to stand on either side were decimated in the earthquake, and there are now large tracts of land on which only pieces of ruin and rubble stand. The end walls that do stand, though, provide a great canvas for popular murals. One very close to the hotel depicts the history of Nicaragua in artistic form. The life of the Indians is shattered by the bloody conquest of the Spanish, the British occupations, and finally the American intervention. In between each of these bloody scenes Nicaraguans are depicted struggling for independence and economic betterment, and in the midst of these is the soon-to-be-familiar symbol of Sandino's hat, a shape that has become synonymous with the Nicaraguan struggle for self-determination and a better life.

This avenue houses many of the most important government buildings, and the newly-built international press centre. Further down there is the eternal flame lit to the memory of Carlos Fonseca, a Sandinista leader who died before what the FSLN refer to as, simply, 'the triumph'. The flame is in a park full of benches, children's activities and

9

wildly luscious tropical flowers. A new basketball ground is in constant demand and is floodlit to allow it to be used at night. And the stalls sell drinks. The Spanish influence is pervasive, in that sense of rambling and relaxing in the evening after a day of battling with the sun.

Near to the ruins of the cathedral you can see two images of Nicaragua almost side by side. One is the Plaza de la Revolucion, where I later attended a May Day March along with 35,000 Managuans. It was a day of genuine celebration with flags and banners, people marching with their schools, factories or militia groupings. There were lots of bands, and people stopped to dance with each other and with passers-by quite regularly. Between the speeches in the square people formed human pyramids. The base was six or eight people. On top of their shoulders, another three or four stood and on top, an individual would attempt to stand and wave to the crowd. As soon as this was done, a big cheer would go up, but very quickly the person would tumble down to the ground. Other people would get tossed in the air with a one-two-three, reminiscent of 21st birthday 'bumps'. Everyone would be laughing, unlike the rather sombre demonstrations of the left here in Ireland, where it is judged that laughing and chatting shows a lack of seriousness about the issue. The Nicaraguans are serious about the issue of their freedom, but they don't have to prove it 24 hours a day. And that's what makes for those moments of genuine good cheer amid the pain. May Day is a national holiday, and everyone was enjoying the day off work, eating ice-creams and cold drinks and greeting each other with great cheer and backslapping.

Right next to the Plaza de la Revolucion stands a building reminiscent of Mussolini's new Rome in its white and imperious strength. It seems strangely out of place here in the beating sun. This monument predates the change in Nicaragua. It is a theatre, now called the Ruben Dario theatre, and it was built between the period of the earthquake and that of the Sandinista revolution. Somoza built it with some of the funds that came to alleviate the horrors of the earthquake, and it is now a reminder of the cold-bloodedness of a regime that could think of artistic edifices while tens of thousands lay dead or went homeless. Its huge Doric columns overlook Lake Managua, and the floodlights remind me of a time when a group apart from ordinary Nicaraguans, and quite proud of their élite status, would have swanned in here in lurex, velvet and starched shirts. The theatre is still used, and I went to see a Cuban comic opera there one night. Outside it was a hot sticky night of buzzing insects and busy people. Inside the theatre it was really cold, with air-conditioning at full blast, the inverse of the status symbol that glowing central heating is in Ireland. All the tickets are one price now, but inside, the original ranking is noticeable, with the plushest box set well back from the auditorium — this was set aside for the Somoza family before 1979. On the night I was there, and I'm told generally, the theatre was quite empty. Nicaraguans seem to prefer the more congenial ambience of the ruins of the Grand Hotel, an outdoor theatre, with a natural backdrop provided by the majestic balconies of the hotel destroyed in the earthquake. It reminded me, although on a more intimate scale, of the use of the baths at Caracalla for opera in Rome. Here, shades of a former splendour are enough for a sense of occasion, with the warm air providing the rest of the setting.

Managua is a sprawling city, with areas or 'barrios' stretching for miles on all sides. The city is dominated by a mountain on which is painted the letters FSLN in thirty-foot-high white paint. From anywhere in the city you can see the letters, and gauge roughly where you are. It's a third world city, with the buzzing markets, crammed buses and street-sellers so common throughout the underdeveloped world. But there is an optimism and confidence that makes you feel that here something is different. It was when I started looking at specific changes that I realised just why that good cheer prevailed. Everywhere I went I met Nicaraguans just bursting to talk about their new lives, their tiredness of the war and the fear they had lived with previously.

The Church of Sancta Maria de Los Angeles is a glass and concrete tent set in the poor barrio of Riguero. In the 1984 election the FSLN received a very high vote here, and it was an area that delivered some of the earliest insurrectionary blows to the Somoza dictatorship before 1979.

The mass held here on a Sunday evening at 5 o'clock is the famous Misa Campesina, and the band belting it out on the altar were among the finest I heard the whole time I was in Nicaragua. Around the walls of the church were twelve to fifteen foot tall murals spelling out the parts of the Catholic tradition which were in sympathy with the poor. Luis Antonio Velasquez was a nine-year-old child martyr who used to sing rebel songs in his local church. He was shot by members of Somoza's National Guard. This is graphically illustrated by use of the symbolism of David against Goliath. The weak and powerless, with justice on their side, can defeat the might of the strong and powerful. Elsewhere, the agonies of Christ are shown to be at the hands of the rich, while it is the poor campesinos who finally deliver his resurrection. There is a painting of the late Archbishop Romero of San Salvador, who is a figure of some importance throughout the Latin American church. He had tried to place the Salvadorean church at the disposal of the poor in the fight for their rights. He was shot dead by members of the Salvadorean militia, while saying mass.

The sermon of Padre Molino on the Sunday I went was an interesting contrast of the gospels of Luke and Matthew in describing the eight beatitudes. While Luke states starkly 'Blessed are the poor', Matthew fudges: 'Blessed are the poor in spirit'. It struck me that the latter version was favoured in the schools and churches in Ireland.

# The Core of the Revolution

Although I had no transport of my own in Nicaragua, I covered a lot of ground. You would never be left waiting long hitchhiking; most vans and trucks will pick up a dozen or more people at a time. And that includes military trucks. Only when going through the centre of the country, where the Contras had their bases in the jungle, would the army be slow to pick up passengers. They were afraid the civilians would be targeted in that situation. Most places are easily accessible, such as the old Spanish governmental seat of Granada, with its colonnades and courtyards, its parks and marble stairways, and Masaya, the centre for Indian crafts, where beautifully-coloured threads are embroidered on every sleeve and cuff. Near here stand the volcano of Masaya and one of Somoza's old prison fortresses, now disused. This is built on top of a steep hill, to prevent escape, and it was here that ten or twelve prisoners were held in each cell, with barely room to lie down. To the north is Leon, a fine old university town. Leon was one of the first towns to join the Sandinista rebels and remains staunchly pro-FSLN. Further north lies the dry and inhospitable land of Chinandega, centre of the cotton region. And far away is the Atlantic coast, accessible only by boat and populated by Nicaragua's Caribbean English-speaking people.

A typical journey I made was to the remote island of Ometepe, a volcanic island in the centre of Lake Nicaragua. This lake is the only fresh-water lake in the world where sharks live, though luckily I didn't spot any. I had decided to spend Easter there, and had been given a loan of a house by a Scottish friend who worked as a midwife on the island; she had gone home for a few weeks. Arriving at the port on Holy Thursday after a cheery jaunt from Managua I joined the queue in the open air at just after nine. The boat was due to arrive from the island about ten, and the return journey would start at eleven. The sun got hotter, and the shaded spots got smaller until we were like a sun-dial, our complete exposure to the heat letting the world know it was getting close to twelve. Word finally arrived that the driver of the boat had been celebrating Easter early and was drunk on the island; the boat was not coming. The next day was Good Friday, so there would be no boat. The only thing to do was to come back on Easter Saturday. I wondered about the people trying to get off the island that day; their frustration must have been much greater than mine. There's no point in trying to rush in Nicaragua, and since I was under little pressure that weekend I decided to wait until Saturday.

The boat trip happened on Saturday all right, although the crossing was rough. You had to cross a wavering plank to get from shore onto the boat, a feat I could only accomplish more or less by going on my hands and knees. The locals were very deft at it, though, and I saw even old people trundle across laden down with packages, food and presents for the holiday weekend. The boat was a small fishing vessel with some room under cover, but most people were out on deck. About half-way across the real sea-sickness struck, and I found myself, along with eight or nine Nicaraguans, heaving over the side of the vessel. The craggy point of Ometepe volcano got closer.

The island itself is very typical of Nicaragua. It is very poor, with only one main road that a car could drive on. Along the waterfront cattle and horses cool themselves at the water's edge, while local people throw themselves into the water fully dressed and wander out again nonchalantly. The formality of a swim in Ireland, getting undressed, into swimming togs, a swim, followed by thorough drying and dressing, is a different world. Despite their closeness to the sea Nicaraguans are very poor swimmers, a fact put down to fear and superstition about drowning. I recall hearing similar stories about fishing communities in Ireland, that it was felt that learning to swim was a temptation to fate. If the sea wants you, you're gone anyway.

This is rural Nicaragua, and although the gains made in the northern regions are not apparent, there is room and freedom not available in the cities. The children are barefoot, but there is no hunger. Rice and beans are served in wooden bowls in the houses I visit, and there are mangos and grapefruit in abundance. Pork and beer, special treats, were kept aside for Easter Sunday, and there was a religious procession through the village street with a local man dressed in white as the risen Christ.

My friend, the Scottish midwife, was attached to a health education programme on the island, specifically aimed at traditional midwives. Before the education programme began one of the midwives used to tie a rope around the delivering mother's waist, to make sure the baby moved down and not up. Another midwife asked about the fitting of an IUD (intra-uterine device): was it necessary to remove a woman's womb to insert one, and if so, how did one go about surgically replacing the womb? But it was not a case of Kate coming from Scotland to pooh-pooh such ignorance. The national health service was addressing this uneven understanding of health throughout the country, and providing primary health training where doctors were in short supply. Role-model dramas were used by the health workers to discuss their reactions to childhood illnesses, labour complications and use of available medicines. As the health workers grew in knowledge and confidence, they were able to distinguish between situations they could deal with themselves, and those requiring a doctor. Such basic medical knowledge, spreading as it is through the isolated countryside of Nicaragua, is helping thousands of lives to be saved, and bringing about a reduction in the grinding acceptance of regular ill-health.

Sometimes in Nicaragua, especially when you had been chatting to local people, and perhaps having a laugh, you'd forget just how far away you were, how different life is in the tropics. I was struck by this entering the house of my friend, who had been away for five or six weeks. She had warned me that the house would be dusty, being the dry season, but nothing prepared me for the carpet of dust everywhere in the house. Every surface, every crevice was covered with a layer of dust some inches thick. It was like a film scene of a hundred-year-old haunted house, with dust clinging to the coverings on the furniture. But this was much, much thicker. No sooner had I begun the process of washing down the floors than the next-door neighbour and her children arrived, and with barely a word started to clean and sweep along with me. It's one of those really clear images of warmth that I was glad to carry home with me.

Another trip that I made left a strong impression of the country's determination and sense of change. Thirty-five kilometres north of Esteli, in the heart of the war zone, lies Condega. It follows the pattern of most Latin villages, a church overlooking a little park, and houses spreading down to the river. The town's only hospedaje or hostel is a sprawling ancient building, housing some Nicaraguan families permanently and some passers-through like myself. A demented old lady is chasing chickens up and down the corridor. Women are scrubbing clothes in the leafy courtyard and laying them flat to dry. A man from the Atlantic Coast proffers his hand and says, in perfect English, 'You're very welcome to Condega'. He works for a meat-exporting company and explains that the main problem in the area is Contra bands rustling cattle, or just butchering young animals. In 1979 many of the big cattle-ranchers herded their stock across the border to Honduras. The attempt to rebuild the national meat industry is constantly being undermined by sabotage and the killing of young cattle. While the man is chatting to me there is a constant procession of wayfarers, filling water bottles, standing at corners to look, brushing their teeth in the big sink. They all give the hostel a general air of run-down eccentricity.

On top of the hill which overlooks the town stands a strange monument — a plane, belonging to Somoza's hated personal guard, which was shot down in the period preceding what's known as 'the triumph'. In early 1979 a troop of the National Guard went on the rampage in the town, in an exercise that was by no means exceptional. They wrecked many people's homes, and at the end of the day, they kidnapped a twelve-year-old girl. They took her away to a place where she was raped repeatedly. The people of Condega, in anger, rallied to the Frente Sandinista, and the townland was the first to be liberated in 1979. For over a month the people waited to see if the rest of the country could oust the Guardia. If they didn't, their little village would feel the full brunt of the spurned anger of the regime. The red and black flag which flew so early over their town was a direct challenge to Somoza's government, one which would be remembered. With great relief came the 19    July.

These northern remote areas remain the most stalwart supporters of the Sandinista government. Every house proudly flies its small flag or carries a picture of Carlos Fonseca or Che Guevara. Back at the hostel a group of Californians tell me that their town is twinned with Condega. Last year they came down and said (as only Americans can) 'O K , whatever you want for your town we're going to get it for you, so what's it to be?' The reply was simple and unanimous — an alarm system, so that the soldiers in the hills could alert the town to an impending Contra attack. I thought of all the facilities a little place like this needs; this choice was a political statement. They were not going to be overrun without a fight. So the Americans spent a fortnight installing the system. And they'd added a facility to broadcast music around the town from the local Frente Sandinista office, a kind of tannoyed local radio. I'm sure the older townspeople cursed this 'addition'.

The next day I went to witness a strange reunion. Near Condega, just sixty years ago, one of Sandino's famous battles against the invading Yankee marines took place. Paul Lory was one of those marines, and Colonel Jose Mergaza was one of Sandino's commanders. The American soldier had thought long and hard about the intervention then and now, and was opposed to its continuance. He wanted to come back, to make amends and to return documentation taken out of the country at the time. The meeting took place in Mergaza's house, and the two men, both hard of hearing, chatted excitedly about the battle of Bromadora, as though

17

the correct strategy was of life-saving importance. 'How many men did you really have on the left flank?' and 'Why did you not attack us when you spotted that opening?' — the kind of questions those of us reared under the shadow of the nuclear bomb find naïve. Colonel Mergaza explained that Sandino's tactic of guerilla fighting meant making the strike and then withdrawing, not closing in to finish off any one regiment. This would have been too costly. After making their attack, they had withdrawn, leaving the Americans to hit at straw, to Puerto Cabezas on the eastern Atlantic coast. There were other battles to fight there.

As I left the room that day Paul Lory, now in his eighties, was singing a little Spanish ditty he had learnt in Nicaragua all those years ago. The marines who had been in these parts in the 1920s had had a reputation for brutality, and for terrorising the local people. The Californians, who had organised the trip, asked Paul Lory about this. He said that his squadron had never been involved in harassment of the local villagers. We debated among ourselves whether this was an oversight of the years, or whether it was indeed other marines who had been guilty of these acts. But the local Nicaraguans, whose families had suffered those attacks, never raised them. In courtesy and kindness they welcomed back this former invader, now come as a wiser friend.

A street vendor laughs cheerily while her t-shirt declares in English 'Don't touch my thermostat'.

# In Search of the General

Niquinohomo is the home of Nicaragua's father, General Sandino. 'I will die with the few who accompany me, because it is preferable to die as rebels rather than live as slaves'. In many ways both the rhetoric and the reality of Nicaragua's guerilla struggle is reminiscent of Ireland's. The small band of mobile troops attacked the occupying forces and withdrew. They depended on the support of the local farmers, without whose supplies they would certainly have starved. And they made the business of staying less and less attractive, forcing an accommodation with local elements who would guarantee the safety and stability of investments, without a direct colonial involvement. Sandino forced the withdrawal of the American marines in 1933. They were replaced by Anastasio Somoza Garcia and his US-trained National Guard.

At the end of the last century, Sandino first drew breath in this neat and picturesque little town. The day I visited, it was the 53rd anniversary of his death and the people of the town had been busy touching up slogans and repainting housefronts for the occasion. The village graveyard was the brightest and most colourful I've seen (I admit to a curiosity that makes me visit them at home and abroad), but Sandino is not buried there. After he was murdered by the Guardia his body was never found. The people were deprived of a martyr's grave to cherish and mind.

He was the non-marital son of one of the town's most influential figures. His mother, who came from indigenous Indian stock, was an employee in his father's company.

Sandino lived with his mother in real poverty until his ninth birthday, and worked alongside her on the big coffee plantations to earn a survival pittance. But it was to the town's biggest house that the young Sandino came, a cool building of polished floors and mahogany furniture built in a square around a luscious courtyard. He joined his father's marital family in what, even at the time, must have been an unorthodox acceptance of progeny outside the marital bed. I wonder about his mother's feelings. She must have felt strongly that he would get a much greater chance in life by leaving her home. After seeing him through those hard and frightening first years she was prepared to sacrifice the enjoyment of the early adult years to give him a chance. And it was probably the contrast between the poverty he had known and the comfort which now surrounded him which led him at that young age to question the inevitable drudgery and unchanging nature of many people's lives.

His former home is now a museum to his extensive battles and travels through Nicaragua in the late 1920s, making life uncomfortable for the occupying American marines. But like many another guerilla fighter his memory has ossified into an image of untarnished greatness. One aspect of his life has become the total. I was interested to hear from the lips of his old girlfriend what kind of person Augusto Sandino really was. I wandered up the road to the run-down shop where Maria Soledad lives.

She's eighty-six now, still lively and clear in her mind. Her face is moulded deep with the lines of drying sun and air. Her smile is one of genuine welcome as she ushers me into a darkened kitchen-cum-shop. The items still available to Nicaraguan shopkeepers fill the shelves — twine, rat poison, fruit. 'I was engaged to marry Augusto from the time I was sixteen and he was nineteen', she told me. Her father refused to allow the marriage to go ahead because *he* was too young. From the pictures she had, he must have looked pretty striking at the time. Though small in height he had very bright blue eyes, light hair and a feel for dressing well. Maria decided it was worth waiting for him to 'come of age'. In the meantime he went away. As Carlos Fonseca puts it in his biography, *Long Live Sandino*, he 'does not feel at ease in his home territory, and like thousands of other Nicaraguan youths he crosses the border, leaving behind in Niquinohomo his sweetheart, Soledad, and his beloved homeland occupied by the blond invader'.

He returned a few years later and was involved in business, transporting beans to Managua for sale. According to Maria, his business partner swindled him by selling him a cargo of rotten beans. Sandino discovered this when he arrived in Managua, drove back in a temper and confronted the 'colleague' in the village square. He was knocked to the ground and reacted by pulling a gun and shooting his erstwhile associate, wounding him. He had to flee the area and the country.

The commonplace division between private and public life began. In Central America, Mexico and for a time North America, Sandino learnt about political struggle. He worked for American multinationals, and saw the beginnings of trade union organisation. In Mexico the peasants told him about the recent struggles of the guerilla warrior, Emiliano Zapata. At home, Maria waited and cherished the letters in which he asked her to wait for him.

Five years later, he wished to return home. He asked his father, who had a lot of power in the town, to arrange a peace with the man he had injured so rashly in his youth. But his father refused to exercise his influence. He warned him that the man he had shot was now mayor of the town, and his brother was in charge of the police. He did not advise him to return to Niquinohomo. I had to smile a bit as Maria Soledad painted this human picture of the great man. It does not take from the courageous fight he was to make against US intervention in Nicaragua; it just places his feet on crumbly campesino earth rather than on perfect slabs of white marble.

From May 1926, when he returned to Nicaragua, Sandino began his guerilla strategy. He covered thousands of kilometres travelling from his base in the northern mountainy regions of the country, across the jungle, to the famous Atlantic Coast and towards the centre of the country where he defeated government and Yankee troops in several decisive battles. 'He had to take on the battle against the invaders of our country', says Maria Soledad, 'exactly as we have to continue today to maintain our country's freedom against the American involvement.' It's stated so simply, and where you would least expect to find radical rhetoric, from an eighty-six-year-old townswoman eight-year-old grand-niece restlessly nudging at her knee.

Over the next seven years, the 'general', as he had become known, led as many as 800 troops in various assaults. In 1927, at the age of thirty-two, he sealed his new life per-marrying a young Segovian, Blanca Arauz, a telegraph messenger for the guerillas. 'I couldn't believe it when I heard', said Maria, with genuine emotion still. 'The shock nearly killed me. I had waited all the time for him to come back. I decided there was no one else for me and that I would spend the rest of my life minding my parents and the children of my sister. I would never marry anyone else.'

It was sad to think of this division and heartbreak caused by the different paths their two lives took, she in the private and tiny world of Niquinohomo, Sandino in the northern hills making a stand for Nicaragua's sovereignty. Although she agreed with that stand, it was rare indeed for women to involve themselves in military struggle at that time. She was twenty-nine and alone, 'let down by first love'. Life continued of them.

It was 1933 before the guerilla army forced the US marines to withdraw. It was an important victory for the Army for the Defence of the National Sovereignty of Nicaragua. Sandino afforded himself the luxury of a visit home, where he called to Maria Soledad's house to ask her forgiveness for deserting her. Women are so often pushed to the sidelines of history, and have no option but to accept being left behind. 'His revolution had been victorious', she smiled without any trace of bitterness. 'I'm left here to tell the story, because all of his family have now died, the "General of Free Men".'

It is not surprising that Sandino has become the symbol for this somewhat maverick revolution, where the emphasis is on self-determination. The philosophy and economics are eclectic, emphasising political pluralism and a mixed economy where there are still opportunities for the rich to get richer in the private sector. It sometimes looked to me like a tiny welfare state attempting to implant itself in a third world economy. And so many people, from liberals to Marxists, from woolly-headed anti-authoritarians to Social Christians, have found a place for their ideology under the banner of 'Free country or death'.

The new National Guard, which now indirectly represented US interests in the country and had been trained by the US army, was placed under the leadership of Anastasio Somoza Garcia in 1934, the first of the three Somoza dictators. His first task was clear. He told a council of Nicaraguan officials in February 1934: 'I have come from the United States Embassy where I have had a conference with Ambassador Arturo Bliss, who has assured me that the government in Washington supports and recommends the elimination of Augusto Cesar Sandino for considering him a disturber of the peace of the country'[1]. In that same month Sandino accepted a dinner invitation to the presidential palace, ostensibly to discuss Nicaragua's future. On his way home, he was murdered. He was thirty-nine years of age.

1. Quoted in the *Central America Fact Book*, by Tom Barry and Deb Preusch, Grove Press Inc., 920 Broadway, New York, p. 272.

*Kate Hughes*

Women wear white scarves to represent a member of their family killed by the Contras.

23

# The Men with the Size 15 Boots

The little wooden shanty was in a mess. Pictures from the walls were scattered on the floor. Furniture was upturned. The kitchen press was knocked over, and earthenware mugs and plates lay broken. In the corner an old lady, who herself looked the worst for wear, was trying to comfort a small weeping child. This family was a very minor victim of the Contra war.

That morning, an explosion had rocked the tower providing electricity to the whole of Managua. It was part of the Contra strategy of hitting industrial and economic targets, in order to run down the Nicaraguan economy. They did not succeed in their aim of cutting off the electricity supply, but they had devastated the houses of a group of poor urban families who lived in wooden constructs near the tower. The danger to these civilians was a side issue. It was another day of war in Nicaragua.

To the north of Nicaragua lies Honduras, and to its south Costa Rica. From these borders come the Contra foot soldiers, rested and fed and ready to begin their attacks on Nicaraguan towns and villages. The Nicaraguan government claims they are a mercenary army, and this is true insofar as they are supported by funding from the US administration. They have been called the 'Nicaraguan Resistance' by the US State Department and in some Western reports but they differ from, say, the resistance movements in Guatemala or El Salvador in being trained in US military camps and supplied with their material needs from outside. This is not to say that there is no discontent within Nicaragua — and clearly among the Miskito population the Contras did find a recruiting ground — it is merely to say that the primary motivation and organisation of the Contra movement is not indigenous to Nicaragua. Without US and private individual backing, they could not have made the military impact which they have. Keeping 15,000 troops armed, fed and mobile costs big bucks, and that is precisely what the Contras have.

In Honduras, just north of the border with Nicaragua, there is a no-go territory in which the Contras have total control. They move freely, unhindered by the Honduran army, and return to US camps within Honduras for training and recreation. On the Nicaraguan side the border is spotted with tiny villages, which have been the main victims of Contra raids and attacks. The north western part of Nicaragua is the most war-torn area in the country and interestingly, it is here in Nueva Segovia that support for the FSLN is strongest.

Many of the Contras are former members of Somoza's National Guard, or people who had some of their property confiscated in the redistribution of agricultural land. In this sense they are more than a mercenary army. They are people with a hatred of the new Nicaragua, and a venom towards those who stayed to work in it. Scottish lawyer Paul Laverty, who has been studying human rights abuses by the Contras, told me about the violence he had seen against ordinary villagers, even children and old people. The methods of torture used are often barbaric. One common abuse is to pierce the tongue of a captured peasant and lead him around by a rope put through it. Christopher Dickey's book, *With the Contras*, shows again and again a boastful macho brutality which permeates both the leadership and foot soldiers of the Contra fighters.[1] Some campesinos have been drawn into the Contra army by poverty and hunger. The money is very good by Nicaraguan standards, with ordinary Contras receiving 25 to 50 dollars a month. For the camp leaders and officers, it becomes a really lucrative business, with good pay, travel and endless funds coming in. A lot of the funding voted to the Contras has gone astray and not been accounted for. In fact, the really bitter internecine disputes of 1987 and 1988 within the Contras were more to do with where the money had gone than anything else. The Contras as a movement are in danger of self-destruction from over-financing.

Paul Laverty told me about a trip he made to Waslala in the north of the country. A Catholic priest had been kidnapped by the Contras and his parishioners feared for his life. Paul went to negotiate his release along with the local villagers. He was shocked by the distance between these Contras on the ground and their leadership, safely havened in Miami. While the leadership spoke of ideological opposition to the Sandinista government, the Contra in Waslala were not aware of their own leaders, and had no interest in ideas or politics. It mattered little to them whether they killed the priest or freed him. Again, there was a frightening nonchalance concerning issues of life and death. After seeing Paul's international legal credentials, and the number and mood of the priest's congregation, they acceded to his release. They were completely obsessed with the weapons they had, the strikes they had made, and the camaraderie of war for its own sake. These sort of encounters make it hard to believe that a political settlement can really demobilise this army. Only a cutting-off of their funds will do that. They will be forced to make new accommodations, to think of work, of returning to Nicaragua to live or settling elsewhere. But as long as the funding keeps coming the war games will continue, with their lethal consequences.

There is some support for the Contras in the isolated centre of Nicaragua, near Boaco and Chontales. This is traditionally a very conservative area, and until recently it was barely touched by the changes since 1979. The only real indigenous support for the Contras which I was able to witness was among a number of Miskito Indian groups. Their discontent is an historic one, although the Nicaraguan government has made some crucial mistakes with regard to them. The Miskito Indians inhabit the eastern Atlantic coast and they have been in the past the most oppressed of all Nicaraguans. The gold and other metals mined in the region were quickly exported back to Britain in the days of British rule, leaving the region completely undeveloped. To this day there are no roads in this north-eastern region, and contact with the capital is by boat transport. The Miskito Indians, cut off from modernisation and economic development, continued to live a primitive existence, their livelihood derived from fishing in the river Coco and from basic tillage.

Back in 1981, when the Contras stepped up their attacks (there were 96 separate border incidents in this area in early 1981), many isolated communities were moved inland for their safety. In January 1982 the government decided to move the Miskito Indians inland, and away from their beloved Rio Coco. To quote Oxfam's Diana Melrose: 'The Miskitos understandably resented the suddenness of their removal and the loss of their homes and crops, which were destroyed to prevent their being used by the Contra. About 10,000 Miskitos fled north across the border, some of them subsequently joining the counter-revolutionary forces. Whilst criticism must be made of the handling of the situation, Oxfam feels that genuine efforts were made to help the 8,000 or more Miskitos who were settled inland'.[2]

The Nicaraguan government fully acknowledges the mistake it made in forcibly moving this population. They themselves provided the grounds for substantial Contra recruitment in this region, and they have spent the period since 1983 trying to make up for their action. They have held talks with the Indian Contras, the Misurasata, leading to an amnesty and the return of many of these fighters. They have instituted a process of autonomy for the east coast. They have written into the new Constitution safeguards for the language and traditions of the Miskito Indians and the other racial groups on the Coast. They have pledged the reinvestment of profits from the mines for the development of the region, and they have facilitated Miskitos who wished to return to the river Coco with resettlement grants. To a large extent these policies have paid off. Even in the last year, several thousand Miskitos have laid down their arms and returned home. A substantial portion of the Miskito Contra movement is now involved in peaceful talks and in the new regional self-government.

The southern front of the Contra war was on the border with Costa Rica. Here, the FDN (Nicaraguan Democatic Force) troops who were also based in Honduras were joined by the forces of the ARDE (Democratic Revolutionary Alliance). Their leader was Eden Pastora, a former Sandinista and leader of the 1972 assault on the National Assembly. I met Pastora in Costa Rica in late 1986. I was brought by one of the ARDE handlers to a large house in the suburbs of San Jose. The porch and hallway were full of rather disgruntled men of massive bulk — Pastora's bodyguards. I was searched and ushered into a sunny room with great baskety chairs. The largest one, I was told, was Pastora's. I could sit anywhere else. On the walls were two photographs, one of Pastora with his troops in the hills. In their green camouflage uniforms they sat laughing. The other photograph was a huge blow-up of Eden as he would have looked ten years ago, thin, bearded and messianic, looking beyond the camera to a point in the distance. The man who came in to shake hands was quite different from this image. Stocky, clean-shaven and middle aged, it was nevertheless clear that Pastora had a certain charisma.

He had just decided to abandon the fight and lay down his arms. He blamed the CIA for his decision. 'I am a Nicaraguan nationalist,' he said. 'I have no time for the Sandinistas because they get support from the Soviets and Cubans. But neither will I be told what to say or do by the Americans. They forget that I am a proud Nicaraguan, a leader of my country.'

During the insurrection period Pastora certainly was among the top leaders of the FSLN. He was strong on military strategy and a key fighter. He undertook and led many of the most daring military initiatives of the early 1970s, of which the assault on the National Palace is the most famous. A number of Somoza's deputies were held hostage and were traded for the release of Sandinista prisoners, and the distribution of food to Nicaragua's poor. It was a brilliant stroke, and one that worked to the great credit of Pastora and his team. The prisoners were set free, the people received the food with great cries of support for the Sandinistas and not a drop of blood was shed.

But Pastora was not considered to be politically astute. The FSLN were aware, after coming to power, that they were going to be under a lot of pressure to give it up. They needed tacticians, diplomats and people with rock-solid political philosophy as leaders. They did not appoint Pastora to the nine-man directorate of 'commandantes' on July 19th. He became extremely disgruntled and fled south, where he began fighting his erstwhile comrades with US backing. Nicaraguans felt betrayed and let down when Pastora went to Costa Rica. 'How much did you get for your hero's medals, Eden?' cries a slogan on several walls in Managua today. The message sums up a feeling that Pastora and his old reputation have been bought by American gold.

Some of that hurt and anger is exemplified in the Museum of Heroes and Martyrs in Managua. Here photographs and newspapers chronicle the period of struggle up to 1979. Where Eden Pastora's face appears, he is not mentioned in the captions. I was a bit worried by this, seeing reflections of Stalinist photo-touching. I approached the guide in the museum to ask who *that* man was. 'Oh, that's Eden Pastora', he said. He shook his head. 'He's no longer on our side'.

He is not viewed as a lost leader any more, just someone who expected personal glory from the Sandinista triumph and couldn't settle down to the routine work of rebuilding Nicaragua. Certainly, as he bantered away, making flirtatious remarks along with stories of his glories and triumphs, he seemed like a dangerously spoilt little boy who wanted everything his own way. The tragedy was that he had been prepared to kill innocent civilians to get it. He had not been happy with the position he was offered in the new government back in 1979, and decided to form a military opposition. But now that particular game was over. His parting shot was: 'Yes, I've definitely given up the war. I want to spend time with my wife and children.' This remark was accompanied by a wink and a laugh. Towards the end of 1988 Pastora was named as one of those joining a new grouping of the internal opposition in Nicaragua, who supposedly 'reject violent means'. They include Erich Ramirez of the Social Christian party, and various factions of the Liberal party.

Pastora seemed cynical of CIA manoeuvres to bring about a united Contra movement. He saw it as an attempt to undermine his personal power and his independent army, ARDE. The CIA, on the other hand, was not interested in personalities. It was interested in winning. And one movement gave the best chance of doing that. 'They know nothing of what we Nicaraguans want,' said Pastora, 'They don't think about us at all. We're just there to carry out their wishes. When I was in the hills on the southern border of Nicaragua we used to get CIA supply drops. Boots of size 15. And huge underpants, made for American GIs. They didn't even remember that Nicaraguans are small people'. At this he laughed.

The CIA had had enough of Pastora, his frivolity, his independence, even, in a strange way, his brand of Nicaraguan nationalism. They stopped funding him. Around this time Pastora was wounded in an attempt on his life, at a press conference given by him at La Penca in Costa Rica. While the US were quick to condemn the attack as a Sandinista one, Pastora himself denied this and remained convinced that he was targeted by the Americans. One way or the other, the party was over.

One man who thought the CIA was wrong to stop funding Pastora was former US General John Singlaub, now president of the World Anti-Communist League. I met him in San Jose, Costa Rica; he had flown in to try to prevent the Pastora split from the Contras. He was a frightening-looking man, head shaved, small and thin with cold steely eyes that looked past whoever he was talking to. Here was a man with a mission. He had been with the Green Berets in Korea, in Vietnam, in the Philippines, ensuring the survival of the American way. 'The target is the Sandinista regime', he said. 'We have to be prepared to use all methods and personnel available to us. Pastora has a following in Nicaragua. OK, he doesn't agree with everything the CIA wants. He can be troublesome. He can ignore the bureaucracy. This is what makes him unpopular. I think if he fills out his requisition forms on lavender toilet paper, we should say "fine" and just accept them'. Singlaub's opinion counts. When the US Congress stopped Contra financing back in 1984, he was able to raise 20 million dollars from private backers, and to organise private audiences with President Reagan for the biggest of them (10,000 dollars merited a ten-minute meeting with the president). He was candid about his relationship with Ronald Reagan: 'I would certainly consider that we are quite close, certainly in our aims. When I come back from a trip like this I call the president, and go to see him. He knows that I understand how best to go about ridding Nicaragua of the Soviet-backed regime there. He trusts me.'

These two men struck me, in their different ways, as typical of the stunted emotional growth often evident in men of their ideas. In Pastora, the problem was ego; he had been pampered and encouraged uncritically, demanded the full spotlight on himself, and fed on the adulation of his soldiers. Egalitarianism, while attractive in principle, looked unglamorous and even dull to a man like this; military adventurism was more appealing. Singlaub, on the other hand, was not distracted by such obvious personal pride. He was machine-like, and I had no doubt was ruthless in war and in intelligence strategy. To him, the pleasure was in winning, and he was ideologically very clear about who and what he wanted to win. This was not hearts and minds, it was battles and wars. The stakes were power and control over people's lives, and the survival of a system to which he was absolutely committed. The very existence of a tiny socialist country like Nicaragua was the threat to the system of free enterprise. And so it had to be quashed.

The latest phase of the Contra campaign has seen the penetration of the central jungle area of Nicaragua. They have been under pressure for some time now from the US to hold territory within the country, in order to argue their legitimacy as a political force back in the States. They had no hope of doing this in the highly mobilised northern areas. For example, in 1985 they tried to take the northern town of La Trinidad. They came down from the surrounding hills and overwhelmed the local hospital, but they were quickly repelled by the local reserve militia force, with some help from the Sandinista army, and 250 of them were killed.

They managed to 'hold' the town for only two hours.

And so they changed tack. They began coming in over the border at the underpopulated centre of the country. Then they trekked for thirty days down towards the largely uninhabited area of Boaco. It was near this central area of Nicaragua that the American Eugene Hasenfus was dropping supplies in 1986, when his plane was shot down by a 19-year-old Nicaraguan soldier. As the burly Hasenfus was led to captivity by the young Indian boy, he began spilling the beans. As far as he was concerned he was part of an undercover mission on behalf of his government. He had been with the army in Vietnam, and this was just a continuation of that war. At the same time the US administration was denying that Hasenfus represented it in any way. Yet numerous personnel involved in the supply drop were ex-army and CIA operatives, very close to US policy, if not able to actually prove their direct employment by the US government.

The Contras have managed to set up bases in the jungly centre of Nicaragua. From here they set out on the missions which are claiming more and more civilian victims as they hit at more economic and industrial targets in the large towns and cities of Nicaragua. The Contra war is the biggest political reality in Nicaragua. In 1984 alone, the year of Nicaragua's last general election, over 900 civilians were killed by them. 134 children perished at their hands between 1982 and 1984, while 5,000 children were orphaned by the war in that period.[3] Material damage in 1984 amounted to over a quarter of a million dollars, representing 70% of the annual value of Nicaragua's exports. And there are so many human stories behind those statistics. This one is typical:

> On the morning of December 4, 200 members of the counter-revolutionary FDN (Nicaraguan Democratic Force) ambushed a truck that was transporting 33 volunteer coffee harvesters toward a plantation in the department of Nueva Segovia. The gunfire killed many of the pickets instantly, while others were wounded. Jorge Luis Briones, one of the survivors, said that the Contras drove their bayonets into the throats

of the wounded and then set fire to the truck, burning alive the remaining survivors. Two of these were a peasant woman and her small child. Five days later, in a remote area of the department of Estelí, counter-revolutionaries ambushed a pick-up truck belonging to the Ministry of Agriculture. Its passengers were the technician Manuel Llanes, his wife, and their maid. As Llanes saw the Contras approaching the truck, he told the two women: 'They're probably going to kill me. If you want to save your lives, don't tell them you're my wife or my maid; say that you don't know me and that I was just giving you a ride.' Both women tried to play along, but the maid was unable to help screaming as she saw the Contras cut his wrists and gouge out his eyes before slitting his throat. They found her crying suspicious and decided to kidnap her. Ten days later, in the Atlantic Coast region, FDN forces attacked a Red Cross ambulance, killing a patient and wounding four first-aid attendants.

The massive financial support of the Contra by the US is crucial to understanding their survival. A year after the Sandinista triumph, there were some anti-government attacks, but it is noteworthy that while nine literacy workers were killed by political assassination in the period March to July 1980, more literacy volunteers were killed in that period by drowning (19), illness (10) and road accidents.[4]

The real escalation of the war began in 1980, after Ronald Reagan became president. The Republican National Convention Platform of 1980 deplored the 'Marxist Sandinista takeover of Nicaragua', and the Marxist 'attempts to destabilise El Salvador, Guatemala and Honduras'. In 1981 credit for trade was withdrawn and a seven million dollar loan from the US Agency for International Development was suspended. Ronald Reagan personally pushed a plan for 19 million dollars of military aid, to be administered by the CIA, to set up a 500-strong army for attacks in Nicaragua. Over the next four years, 100 million dollars of official aid was given to the Contras by the US Congress, and another 100 million dollars was voted in July 1986.[5] In addition, private backers contributed nearly another 100 million dollars, while the surreptitious sale of arms to Iran accounted for 12 million dollars, and Saudi Arabia a further 30 million dollars. The Saudis claim that this contribution was at the personal request of President Reagan. They did not feel in a position to refuse.

Development projects have been declared primary targets in the war. Ben Linder, the young American citizen killed in April 1987, was working on a hydro-electric project to provide light to remote villages. Britain's medical journal, *The Lancet*, pointed to attacks on the campaign to eradicate infectious diseases. 'Several anti-malarial workers and many volunteers have been killed by Contras. Their disruption of the health system and communications and attacks on peasants have resulted in new malaria problems. It appears that only a termination of hostilities will make it possible for the border areas to achieve the successes in malaria control noted in the rest of the country.'[6]

In an attack on the northern town of Pantasma in late 1983, 47 people were killed, and these included six teachers burned to death in the Ministry of Education building. Agricultural machinery and a good distribution centre were burned to the ground. Although a basis has been laid for real structural change in Nicaragua since 1979, as long as attacks like these continue, no real improvement can occur in people's daily lives. The disbanding of the Contras remains the basic priority.

1. C. Dickey, *With the Contras*, Simon and Schuster, 1985.
2. Diana Melrose, *Nicaragua: the Threat of a Good Example*, Oxfam 1985.
3. *Envio*, Vol. 4, issue 43, Jan. 1985, published by the Jesuits at the University of Central America, Managua.
4. *Right to Survive — Human Rights in Nicaragua*, Catholic Institute for International Relations, London, 1987.
5. *Right to Survive.*
6. *The Lancet*, 19   May 1984, p. 1125.

This mother in a northern war zone had already lost her husband and son in the war. Her house had just been destroyed in an attack. 'Here I stand with all I have in the world,' she said.

Paul Laverty

After an attack, a villager whose house lies in ruins behind him immediately starts to rebuild.

# Some Political Debates

I was going to visit two Chilean friends one night and decided, as a lavish treat, to bring some Chilean wine. Nicaragua, being tropical, does not produce wine, and like other imports it is expensive, paid for with scarce foreign currency. The wine sat ostentatiously among my ordinary groceries, but I was feeling quite pleased with myself. This would be a nice surprise, and something special. The man behind me in the queue began to talk to me, asking me where I came from. When I said Ireland, he began to chat away. He knew a lot of detail about the Irish hunger-strikes, about Bobby Sands, about Ireland's historic relationship with Britain. 'It's really a fight for self-determination,' he said. Suddenly, a woman two places behind him, hearing a snatch of what he was saying and presuming he was talking about Nicaragua, started to shout. 'It is not about self-determination, it is about starving people, it is about depriving us of what we need, it is about queues and hardship.' She was a woman of about fifty, with several heavy gold bracelets on each arm, and a thick gold and jewelled necklace at her neck. As she roared at the man, an unholy argument began. They shouted about the shortages and what caused them, about Daniel Ortega and who he represented, about rationing and distribution problems. The rest of the queue joined in with shouts of approval and laughter for the strongest arguments on each side. Then came the inevitable. Pointing to my basket the woman let out a string of abuse. 'Before we could buy what we wanted, now only the gringos (i.e. foreigners) can buy wine'. It was true. Wine was too expensive for most Nicaraguans. But the man, who had told me he was a teacher, quickly retaliated: 'Who could afford wine before the triumph?' he said. 'A tiny handful. Now we concentrate on giving everyone the basics before providing the luxuries for the rich. Hard luck if you lost out.' As I slipped out the door, unseen and mortified, the queue was cheering this point, and goading the woman about where she got her money. The battle of the classes made for spontaneous street fun. And no one feared to state their view of life.

It struck me at the time that people had always debated in this open way in Nicaragua, it seemed so much a part of people's way of relating. But of course that was not the case. Democracy, in the sense of a system without fear of state reprisal, and with a real choice of political candidates is a real newcomer to Nicaragua, barely ten years old. Yet it already seems to be firmly esconced as part of the system and way of thinking.

When the Sandinistas came to power in 1979, they did so as the result of an insurrection. The guerilla movement appears to have had mass backing, and the euphoric pictures of the march into Managua on 19　July certainly suggest a popular excitement at the change. But it wasn't until 1984 that the new government got a chance to test their popularity at the polls. An election was held for a 96-member assembly, to represent all the areas of the country. 'That was the most exciting time', Rosario Lopez, a Managuan street trader, told me. 'For the first time we felt it mattered whether we voted or not, it was like a new game, and we were thrilled. Firstly, all our names were registered, all over the country, and we received cards to vote.'

It is worth remembering that during the forty-five years of rule by the Somoza family, Nicaraguan elections had been synonymous with fraud and corruption. Votes were openly bought with food and alcohol. The day after the election the streets were strewn with drunken men, according to observers from Oxfam. Changing the view and reality of election day was a big job for the new government. Once people were registered, and a voting procedure was adopted (after careful study, mainly of European systems), the most important thing was to ensure real involvement in the election process, and a wide choice of candidates.

From the outset the US administration put great pressure on the opposition to refuse to run in the election. It would suit the view of Nicaragua as a totalitarian regime better, if only one or two parties were to run. Arturo Cruz, leader of the Democratic Co-Ordinating Committee (Coordinadora) (and himself in the political leadership of the Contras at the time), announced the intention of the Coordinadora to boycott the elections. The FSLN took the opportunity of a Socialist International meeting in Rio de Janeiro in October 1984 to open talks with Cruz. Twenty 'Electoral Guarantees' demanded by the CDN, such as more media time and money for paper supplies, were granted by the FSLN representative, Bayardo Arce, in exchange for a genuine ceasefire by the FDN/ARDE troops during the election period. The election would be postponed until January 1985.

At this point Cruz suggested that he might not be able to convince the leadership of the CDN in Managua (consisting mainly of members of COSEP, the Supreme Council of Private Enterprise) to agree to the terms. He sought a general extension of the deadline for the elections, but was able to give no commitments that he could deliver a ceasefire then or at a later date. Arce figured that this was just a stalling tactic, and the talks came to a standstill. This was a big blow to the electoral process. The CDN, despite their close ties with the military forces fighting the government, were seen as the key alliance of groups absolutely opposed to the Sandinistas. Their absence would be noticeable, and their supporters angered.

The FSLN reported openly where the talks had collapsed and how far they had been prepared to go to try to achieve the participation of the CDN in the election. Willy Brandt, the Socialist International president, was in no doubt that a genuine effort had been made. In Managua two weeks later he declared: 'In all electoral processes, only those who want to participate can participate'. And a few days later in Mexico he said: 'Go to Managua and you will see, as I saw, a city covered with electoral campaign posters of different political parties, which are all competing under equal conditions. The sensible thing would have been for Arturo Cruz's group to participate. But the negotiations failed, and that group missed the train.'[1]

It certainly looks as though the CDN never had any real intention of running. Their close ties to the US Embassy, who were advocating a boycott, adds to this impression. But there were still two important, stridently anti-Sandinista, parties in the running, the PCD (Democratic Conservative Party) and the PLI (Independent Liberal Party), along with four smaller parties ranging from Social Christian to Maoist. But the pressure on parties to drop out continued, yielding some results.

In the meantime, talks were opened with all of the parties on the post-election political process. The CDN were invited to these talks also, but did not attend. Everything was organised to guarantee political freedom whatever the election result: there would be periodical elections; people were guaranteed freedom of movement and organisation; the economy would continue to be a mixed one with diverse forms of ownership. The debate on Nicaragua's new Constitution would follow the elections, and all parties would be allocated broadcasting time according to their support in the electoral contest.

Immediately following the signing of these accords, which seemed to set the basis for a fair election and for post-electoral rights, Virgilio Godoy, the PLI president, announced his party's intention of withdrawing from the elections. The party was deeply divided because of the pressure to boycott. In the event the party's vice-president, Constantino Pereira, opposed the abstentionist policy, and called on Liberal followers to vote for the party in the election. This advice was followed by many voters. A similar debate was engineered within the Democratic Conservative Party but their president, Clemente Guido, won the day and the Conservatives remained in the running.

The pressure on the parties of the right seems to have been palpable, and it happened too consistently across the parties to be just an indication of internal debate or pre-election nervousness. I feel it must be said that the United

States administration mounted huge international pressure on these parties. And given that some of them received funding from there (through the National Endowment for Democracy and other agencies) US pressure was important. Nevertheless the elections went ahead with at least a reasonable choice of candidates, spanning the spectrum of right to far left.

'There was great joy on the election day', Rosario Lopez told me. 'There were lots of foreign observers here, and people were helping each other to read election literature. I was supporting the FSLN and it was such a thrill to ask people for a vote, even if they ended up saying no. My mother voted conservative, because she supports the Cardinal [Obando Y Bravo] and we had great times arguing. Some of the older people are afraid it will be hard to get to Heaven if they stand up to the bishops and the Pope. But we younger people want a better life now, and for our children here. Not just in the next life.'

Over seventy per cent of the electorate voted. This is fairly similar to Irish voting at general elections (73 to 76%), but contrasts sharply with the voting rate in the US, where only one-third of the population votes in presidential elections. The FSLN received 67 per cent of votes cast, short of their hoped-for 80%, yet realistic in a situation of war-weariness and economic scarcity. The Conservatives received 14%. Their strongest showing was in Granada, a rich old colonial town. They were weakest in the war zones. The Liberals, who in the end agreed to stand after pressure from their own grass-roots, got 9.7%. Out of 96 seats the smaller parties won 12, 6 for the popular Social Christians, and two each for the Communist Party, the Socialist Party and the Maoist MAPML. The showing of the Sandinistas was strongest in Regions 1 and 2, comprising the northern war-torn areas of Esteli, Nueva Segovia, Leon and Chinandega.

An all-party Irish delegation was among the thousands of politicians from different countries invited to scrutinise the electoral process. The group included Bernard Allen for Fine Gael, Liam Hyland for Fianna Fail, Michael D. Higgins for the Labour Party and Independent Senator Shane Ross.

41

They pointed out that while they were brought to polling stations to see the procedure, they were completely free to drop in unannounced on any voting booth. This they did, and they concluded in their report: 'Members of the delegation are unanimous in their opinion that the elections themselves were carried out with full integrity ... Polling day itself showed a population quietly resolute to carry out the democratic process in an orderly fashion. Some reports on the elections refer to the three small parties (i.e. the CDN) who boycotted the elections as "main opposition parties", and said that their non-participation deprived the elections of all representative value. The delegation found no evidence that these parties had wide support within the country.' La Prensa, the national newspaper which absolutely opposes the Nicaraguan government, was active in the election period. It urged people all through the campaign to boycott the elections, backing the CDN view all the way, and congratulating Virgilio Godoy on his plan to support the boycott. On 5   November, the day after the elections, the newspaper headlines reflected their various editorial positions. The FSLN paper, Barricada, read: 'A Victory For Sandino In Free Elections'. The independent El Nuevo Diario said: 'The People Won', while La Prensa stressed the abstention rate: 'Voting Takes Place With Great Apathy'. A reporter friend of mine smiled when I quoted that headline to her. 'And if the voting had been 99%, that would have been proof that the elections were a fraud', she said.

Democracy in Nicaragua involves more than voting every four years. There is an involvement, an input, directly from the people into important decisions affecting them. The new Constitution, which was promulgated in January 1987, was discussed far and wide. Open meetings involving different sectors were held. The meetings organised by Amnlae, the women's organisation, were an important example. Altogether 40,000 women at 170 venues attended the discussions. It is acknowledged that these were the best attended and most vociferous of all the constitutional debates held. Marisol, a young coffee harvester, described one of the meetings held up in the rural townland of Matagalpa. 'We were all delighted to be there and the men were minding the children. We wanted our right to leave an unhappy marriage written into the Constitution, not just legal divorce. Again and again, some of the women talked about their husbands ignoring them, yet expecting their dinner served up each evening. One woman said these husbands should be kicked out and their wives should start a new life. This got a great cheer. It was a great feeling to be at a meeting together and on our own. There was much more laughter than at a union meeting run by the men. And our point was taken up and included in the Constitution as our right.' Another issue that came out of the women's meetings on the Constitution was a decision to ban the use of women in selling products, and a recognition of the special support owed to the mothers and wives of the martyrs of the revolution, and of the young soldiers mobilised for the Contra war. Problems such as economic shortages and domestic violence also came up repeatedly at the meetings on the Constitution, and they have been the subjects of legislation in the past two years.

It was not only during the constitutional debate that popular democracy was tried . Picture standing for five hours in ninety-degree heat, with the sweat continually rolling down your back, listening to minute points being raised to relevant government ministers and civil servants. This was the picture at a Cara Al Pueblo (Face the People) meeting I attended at an agricultural factory. After an hour I was feeling dizzy, dehydrated and distracted but people were only getting into their stride. I suppose there is a greater tolerance of long meetings where there are not so many leisure distractions, but it was also clear that people were anxious to make their points. They felt they would be acted upon.

One speaker made the point that sometimes their wages were a day late being delivered up from Managua. He wanted to know that he could depend on the money arriving on, say, every Thursday. A woman pointed out that it was very difficult to get doctors to work in the remote rural areas. They wanted to live comfortably in the city, where people could come into their surgeries and they would not have to travel up small roads. The Minister for

Health, Dora Maria Tellez, raised a great cheer when she said that she was aware of this problem and was introducing legislation to ensure that young doctors would spend a number of years after their training in the countryside, to ensure adequate health care throughout the country. A woman got up and said that she had written out her question because she was not used to speaking in public. It concerned the lack of paper for the local school, which, she said with great emotion, was what all they were struggling for was about. She got warm applause and embraces from those around her when she sat down. President Daniel Ortega, chairing the meeting, took notes on all the points raised, and replied to all of them at the end. I was amazed at the stamina that everyone had, and was even more amazed when I heard that a meeting like this one takes place every week in a different venue, with the president attending each one. Given the diplomatic and policy-making workload which the Sandinista government must have, I remember thinking that there must be a strong commitment to keep these 'Face the People' meetings going. Perhaps they feel that they will never completely lose touch with the problems and dissatisfactions on the ground as long as they maintain this kind of forum.

Another Cara Al Pueblo I attended was given over to city business people, who were most concerned about trade, transportation problems and anger at their individual losses in the economic redistribution. Despite the fact that the majority of them were virulently anti-government, this 'Face the People', like all of the others, was broadcast live on radio. The criticisms were faced, evenly, and people could judge for themselves whether the answers given were adequate.

The lack of fear in the new Nicaraguan democracy is palpable. It was brought home to me one day, as I sat squashed into a bus. The US trade embargo has made spare parts impossible to get, and the bus fleet is now less than one-third of its full complement. Instead of passing people by the buses just stop, and everyone inside squeezes in a bit more. Even on long journeys as many as 150 people will be on board a single-decker bus. Bags of shopping, crying children, legs, arms, getting an angle to stay upright, holding your grip, swinging with the bumps. At every stop children and women appear at the windows selling iced fruit drinks in plastic bags. On rural journeys you might have ten or fifteen chickens squeezed in, their legs tied, their eyes staring. On one such journey, I was almost reduced to tears; the heat, the crush, the exhaustion were really getting to me, while all around people bantered and shouted at one another. There was a drunken soldier who kept roaring and singing at the top of his voice, and generally showing off. The women on the bus finally had enough of him. They shouted at the bus-driver to stop the bus and then they ordered the soldier off. My last sight of him was staggering up the road trying to establish his balance, to walk in the blazing heat. I thought this epitomised Nicaraguan democracy today. In what other Latin American country would a drunken soldier allow himself to be put off a bus by a group of women telling him to catch himself on? Indeed, even in Ireland people might be loath to take such a risk. To the women on the bus, a Nicaraguan soldier was not someone to be feared. He was to be told off and taught a lesson, like they'd teach to one of their own sons.

1. *Envio.* Vol. 4, issue 4, Nov. 1984.

*Kate Hughes*

Picking the coffee bean — the backbone of Nicaragua's largest export industry.

# Reporting the War

Journalists converge on certain countries. Clear phone-lines, good hotels, competitive rates for the all-powerful dollar, these are the things that decide where they camp. Back in the early eighties most of the Central American correspondents were in San Salvador; that was where the big story was, and the Camino Real was a damn good hotel. Then the death squads started coming into the hotel, asking for reporters by name and making clear their disapproval of certain stories. The reporters moved *en masse* to Costa Rica.

San Jose, the capital of Costa Rica, is rich and modern. Its cars are new and fast, its hotels modern and air-conditioned. Every product is available. But it's expensive, so the move to Managua began in late 1984. Many reporters came to cover the elections, and stayed. It was possible to live well, cheaply and safely there. Communications were ok in regional terms, and there was no antagonism to journalists. If anything, Nicaragua was so desperate to portray itself as an open society that reporters were treated like nobility. Anything they wanted was made available to them — including information, for those who were so inclined.

War correspondents are a pretty tough, macho bunch. The women among them have a hard time muscling in and having their say. But the life of the press corps is about more than that. It's about those who want the glamour and the invitations meted out to foreign reporters, and it's about those who are into hard work, finding the facts, and analysing their relevance. I met both types in Central America. The lazy ones took feeds, and were prepared to furnish the line being asked for by their editors. The questioners had to fight to get printed or heard, insisting that the analysis came from the facts, and not the dredging up of material to fit the prejudices of an audience back home.

Most of the foreign press corps in Nicaragua worked for American networks and newspapers. This gave a strong bias to what was considered newsworthy. During my time there I worked for NBC radio, and I was told on several occasions that the death of six or eight Nicaraguans in a Contra attack was simply 'not news', whereas the visit of a Republican Congressman to give a ritualistic denunciation of the country was 'of interest'. The language used in war reporting inevitably tells its own story. The resistance to the use of the term 'Nicaraguan government' was palpable. The term 'Sandinistas' or 'Sandinista regime' implied an illegitimacy, without another word. Similarly I found myself in battles, both in print and in broadcasting, about what to call the Contras. The US media had a preference for the terms 'rebels' or 'resistance'. The Nicaraguan press called them 'mercenaries'. Calling them the 'Contras' or the 'the US-backed Contras' was resisted, but it was 100% accurate as a description. Finding the words to describe a politically-charged war is not easy, but it is essential to find accurate terminology to avoid skewing a report before a single fact is submitted. The rows that went on among reporters in Managua about this reminded me of similar arguments in Ireland about the use of the terms terrorist and gunman, murder and killing, and emotionally-charged descriptions like outrage and carnage.

It is nonsense for any journalist to pretend to be completely objective in covering a war or political situation. The very knowledge and insight that the profession allows gives us an insider view of the facts. Editorial pressure always favours the status quo. Most journalists are in some way crusading, hoping that their copy may encourage the powers that be into humanitarian action. Along the way, the pressure of deadlines and the constant exposure to tragedy can kill off any sense of caring; cynicism and a jaded eye take over. 'What's new in the story?' says it all, a reporter who's been on the job too long, and no longer cares what's right or wrong, or more commonly, who's right and who's wrong. Cynicism, as apart from scepticism, is deadly for a working journalist. To be any good you have to have a curiosity about 'the real story', and enough of a pioneering spirit to determine to unmask it no matter what.

I've always felt that the best writers and broadcasters are people who come from a perspective, and who see their work in a historical and political context. Reporters need to be on the side of the underdog, of the individual rather than institutions. The instinct of the establishment is for cover-up. That of the journalist should be to uncover the truth, no matter what the cost to those in high places.

Of course, sometimes the facts that become apparent on investigation show things to be quite in order, or an individual malevolently trying to impugn a person in authority. In that case, ethics and a sense of fair play must ensure that the truth is made known. I think that the only defence those in control in society have against the operation of a truly free press lies in having nothing to fear. That operates against public scandal much more than the supposed objectivity of journalism.

Most of the press corps working in Nicaragua were attached to American newspapers and networks. There is an unspoken pressure in the fact that the US administration is the main financial backer of the Contra fighters. The fact that half the public representatives in the United States believe that Nicaragua is totalitarian and Marxist emphasises the importance of some stories. A demonstration of 700 people who oppose the government is taken as news, while a Mayday rally of 35,000 in support of the Sandinistas doesn't merit a line. This example springs to mind, because these were two stories that I offered to NBC in one week. The first was carried, the second rejected. The duty editors were keeping their audience happy and reflecting popular worry and prejudice.

Many of the American journalists took their responsibilities very seriously. They would spend weeks away from home, trekking into the mountains with the Nicaraguan army or with the Contras, accurately describing the morale and the problems of both sides. They would follow up the victims of Contra violence, investigate economic problems and those in the distribution system, they would visit prisons and tabulate prisoners' problems and complaints. One told me about following the trail taken by the Contras down through Central Nicaragua's jungles. The trail was littered with American hardware, artillery that proved too heavy for the long trek, the gift of the American taxpayer. But this reporter could find no-one to publish this most interesting story. It was too technical, demanded too much thought to figure out why. It was neither gory nor sensationalist enough for the tabloid press, nor significant enough of itself for the 'qualities'. That piece of news never filtered out.

In a country like Nicaragua there is only one story for the foreign press — the war. Not just the casualties and strikes of the military conflict but also the politics, the opposition, the issues placed under the spotlight by the US funders, such as press freedom and economic dissatisfaction, the personalities of the Sandinista leadership, and the possibility of conflicts between them. This gives a small space for journalists to work in. Most of them are paid on a piece basis. Where there is no story for a week, they don't get paid. 'You get worn down', one reporter told me. 'Things you thought you'd never report become stories, because you know they'll be taken up. And that's fifty dollars. You do get greedy.' She was one of the hardest-working reporters in the country, but she had become worn down by the tedium of constant filing. And someone outside the country, who knew less about it was able to decide for her what was 'a good story'.

The weekly round of press conferences dealt with issues not likely to be taken up internationally. The economic plan for the next year, and production targets for exports and consumption, the progress of the autonomy plan for the east coast, the continuing work to clear Lake Managua of pollution — none of these had any journalistic 'sex-appeal'. The war, on the other hand, provided endless copy.

On one occasion I went to a press conference in which nine captured Contras were being presented to reporters. As I watched them being brought in, poorly dressed, some very young, speaking hesitantly, my sympathy was with them. As I noted what they had to say, I was drawn in even more. One young man, with a sensitive face, told how he and others in his village had been forcibly taken northwards, and press-ganged into fighting. Was he saying this to get easy treatment from his captors? Another spoke of the money he got paid, more than his family ever dreamed of. He was able to send home 25 dollars every month to his parents, and this ensured the survival of his younger brothers and sisters.

Then a reporter asked them about the names they had gone by while operating militarily. The oldest of the men, with no trace of regret, announced that his name had been 'El Terror' (Terror) while his second-in-command was known simply as 'El Muerto', The Dead (One). These men could do no damage now, but I began to think of the reactions of unarmed villagers in the northern region whenever they heard these names. The brutality of their raids came into memory, and my sympathy began to wane. An attack just three weeks earlier on a water tower in Managua had destroyed hundreds of small shanty houses, and injured many children and old people. It was a tiny story, not reported outside Nicaragua, but I remembered that the signature 'El Terror' had been left painted among the rubble. A reporter mentioned this, and the Contra agreed that yes, that had been one of their recent operations.

One trip that I took to the war zone was organised by the Ministry of Defence. There had been an attack on a northern village, and three children had been killed. Anyone who wanted to see the damage and talk to the local people was advised to be at the International Press Centre at midnight. I made my way there, filled with trepidation. The room was full of jaded hacks, nearly all men, eagerly trying to show how cool they were about the trip. Danger was a mere occupational hazard. They slapped each other's hands, clapped each other's backs, and laughed uproariously at the merest hint of humour. One boasted that he was 'half shot' and another commented on the heat. 'It was so bad today that you couldn't even have sex — at the vital moment, poosh, out you slipped!' The few women present talked among themselves, or pretended to be buried in newspapers and books. It would be better once we got on the road, with something to occupy our minds.

As we sat into the bus, I thought what a strange way of life journalism is. Employers demand objectivity but know that every reporter has a leaning. The public knows that too, and picks its favourite writers on the basis of agreeing with their 'line' or way of viewing things. But a greater requirement than objectivity is the appearance of nonchalance, that nothing from any side could surprise or shock the journalist. The jaded palates have seen caviar snacks and champagne cocktails, injured children and starving villages, and they must treat both as equally 'normal'. Life goes on, write up the copy and wait for the next assignment, unmoved, unaffected, but still able to sort out the truth amid the mire of distracting signals. Brashness is the commonest trait of the working reporter, and it may be a great help in getting directly to the story commissioned. But it is not the best trait for noticing detail, in being sensitive to situations or in analysing greater trends. Where a fearless arrogance is the primary quality of media workers, the public will be given the fed line, the obvious conclusions and the language of sensation and easy understanding. But here I was, part of this news crew, and we were going to see a village which we were told had just experienced a 'strong attack' that day. I hoped we'd be up to it. At the back of the bus the loud American snored off the alcohol.

The bus was ancient and it banged along slowly up through north west Nicaragua, to Leon, through Chinandega and on to Somotillo, about twenty miles from the Honduran frontier. It was five in the morning, and in the half-light young soldiers could be seen running here and there. Somotillo itself was full of military trucks, parked around the village square, and in every doorway were families already up and working. By six o'clock a ball of orange fire announced sunrise, and we were in military trucks bone-shaking our way up the tiny roads to the border.

In my time in Nicaragua, only once was I hit by a feeling of real dejection and depression among the people. We entered the town next to the now evacuated Santo Tomas, and around the well, pain-lined faces turned to us in desperation and misery. The slogans covering each inch of brickwork told a story of optimism not yet effaced: 'Welcome to the third phase of the agrarian reform', 'The Yankees will be overcome' and 'The people united will never be defeated'. Now they were still, stunned like the people of Pompeii paralysed by sudden lava. They looked wretched and heart-broken, and seemed barely aware of zoom lenses and faded denim staring into their misery. They were thinking of the three children up the way.

A military blackboard explained what had been happening in the previous four days. The area of Santo Tomas, only a few hundred yards from the border, had experienced five attacks by Honduran troops and by shelling from across the frontier. The last mortar hit three children as they walked home to their village, and all three died. This was not a Contra attack, and by all accounts it was a lot 'cleaner' than would have been expected from the more vengeful counter-revolutionaries. Although Honduras is ostensibly a sovereign disinterested neighbour of Nicaragua, in reality it has ceded control of about nine kilometres of its southern territory to about 12,000 Contra troops. They operate openly there, and organise their own policing without interference from the Honduran army. At the same time, Honduras allows US troop manoeuvres to take place in its territory. The proximity of these 'war games' (as they are called) clearly signals to Nicaragua the possibility of invasion. The pay-off for all of this, in classic banana republic terms, is US economic aid. Between 1980 and 1985 what has become known as the 'rain of dollars' showered 572 million dollars on the debt-ridden economy of Honduras. The price of an independent foreign policy, as Nicaragua knows, is the cutting off of this aid, of soft loans, and a diminution of trade. Honduras prefers to play ball rather than suffer these consequences.

So this was no accidental border skirmish. A constant strategy of baiting goes on, and the Nicaraguans are convinced that the US is looking for a local pretext to stage an invasion or large-scale attack. So they don't react militarily. Instead they choose to bring the press to see the damage, and hope for some international reaction. This must be pretty frustrating for the Nicaraguan military, their discipline concentrated on not responding, their officers intent on the painstaking explanation of what happened and how. Unlike the boys' comic version, war is not always about 'zapping' your enemies.

While the military explanation was going on, I noticed in a doorway a young woman dressed in black. She was sobbing brokenheartedly, seeing nothing, wrapped in a private world of shocked grief. Moments later we were brought into the small house where her son and the two other children were laid out in their little coffins. The air was rent with despair. The children's fresh complexions and delicate eyelashes remained young, but the dressed wounds hung with tiny crosses of lace and starched cotton were a grim reminder of their bloody and indiscriminate death. The brother of one of them leaned into the coffin to half-lift his brother, and crying repeated again and again, 'Why him, why do this?' I could understand the desolation evident in that poor village. They were living with the proximity of death.

Back through the town, people studied our reactions. Would we help by what we would write and broadcast? An old woman told me of the fear the community lived with: 'This is an area where we have cleared the Contras,' she said. 'We are so heavily mobilised that they cannot get near us. And then we get showered with bombs from another country. How long will it go on?' I saw only one smile before I left that village: a small infant being washed at the village well shrieked happily as the cold water rinsed her of foamy suds.

We then went out to the evacuated village of Santo Tomas, a pretty little area with benches scattered under trees, and whitewashed buildings. All that now remained in the quiet morning was a gaggle of undisciplined turkeys, and two squealing pigs that were being loaded on to a small truck. Everything else was still. Some rocking chairs still sat outside small cabins, and the school was closed, its desk-chairs stacked in the corner. The Nicaraguan army had declared it could no longer guarantee the safety of the village, and people had moved out *en masse*. Some were now living in the next town in makeshift plywood shelters, others had gone further to stay with relatives elsewhere in the country. The evacuation might last a year or just a few weeks. In the meantime the little possessions of comfort were left behind. Normality was the luxury people prayed for. That morning things were quiet, and the only evidence of hostilities were some craters in the road and near people's houses, and some US-made 120 mortar shells. When it was time to go, one reporter fell behind as we got into the military truck. Another shouted out: 'Hurry up, don't you know we've women waiting in Managua'. They all laughed. For the first time that morning, I felt a real shudder.

Reporting the news was a pretty routine job most of the time. You'd get up in the mornings, scour the newspapers, go to press conferences, attend demonstrations. Then it was a question of phoning copy to the States or to Ireland, and trying to stir up some interest. It's a pretty powerless position to be in, at a great distance from the metropolis where news value and importance is decided. You feel like a begging relative trying to spell out the problems to someone who's only half-listening. You start using buzz words to make an impact, or point out that the wires (the international wire services i.e UPI, Reuters, etc.) are covering the story, which means it's going to be big news the next day. People are egocentric enough to wonder will they miss out if they don't cover what you're offering, and the story runs. On other occasions the distance puts you at such a disadvantage that Nicaragua loses out. I remember once being on to RTE radio offering a story. The producer was hassled, busy and not too interested. At that moment I wished that I could just walk into the studio and explain what was going on face to face. Then I could have made an impression, an impact. Instead I had to accept a refusal.

That particular story was one of the biggest pieces of international news to come out of Nicaragua in 1987. It was the death of Ben Linder, a US citizen working on a voluntary basis on a hydro-electric project in northern Nicaragua. The aim was to provide electricity for some of the remote villages of the countryside. As he knelt beside the river, measuring the flow, the Contras struck. He was killed, along with two Nicaraguan peasants. Buildings were burned, and dozens of local militia members were injured repelling the attack. The area had no Nicaraguan army presence, a fact obviously well-known to the Contra attackers. It fitted very well into their declared policy for 1987 of hitting industrial and development targets. It also fitted the instruction given in the CIA training manual for the Contra forces: 'This is total war at grass-roots level'. Ben Linder was just one of its 20,000 victims. But he was a US citizen, so this was different.

I was sitting at home reading when the news came through on the radio. Within minutes, NBC were on. This story would be very big in the States. They wanted everything I could get on it. Details of the killing, interviews with government personnel, American friends and co-workers, demonstrations at the US embassy, the arrival and words of the Linder family, the funeral. In addition, several US local chat shows rang for me to participate in discussions of Nicaragua in the light of the Linder killing. It seemed the Contras had made a very costly error, in terms of their continued funding.

The Linder family were quiet and impressive. The father was himself a doctor and travelled to the area of the attack to study the post-mortem findings. He told a crowded press conference that it appeared to him that his son had been killed in a pre-meditated way, and not as a chance target in a skirmish. He had been shot in the legs, said Mr. Linder, so he was obviously immobilised. But the fatal wound was delivered at point-blank range, to the head. The US embassy was pressed on what they intended to do, by way of inspection of the body. On the eve of the funeral, the press attaché announced that they would not be travelling to Matagalpa where the body was; it was too difficult a trip and besides, 'the Sandinistas have hijacked the body for propaganda purposes'. He did point out that the region where Ben Linder was working was deemed 'unsafe' for US citizens by the embassy, being part of the war zone. When US ambassador Harry Bergold met members of the US citizens committee, he reiterated this point. 'Ben Linder knew that he was putting himself in danger by being in that region.' He went on to remark that although the death was causing a big stir in the US, it was then only April and a long way to the next vote on Contra aid in September. It was possible that this would have blown over in the intervening months, he remarked.

I attended and covered the funeral of Ben Linder in Matagalpa. The whole town turned out for it. At the front were a group of women carrying purple wild lilies. These were mothers and companions of Nicaraguans killed in Contra attacks. At the graveyard they presented their flowers to the Linder family as a symbol of their common suffering. School children of various ages walked and sang. Others played funeral music, and sang songs of the rebellion period. Mr and Mrs Linder spoke, as did a young American colleague of Ben's. 'His work will continue', she said. President Daniel Ortega spoke of the effects of Contra violence, and pointed to the different internationalists who had died while working in Nicaragua. He thanked the foreign workers who had so selflessly given of themselves for the survival of the new Nicaragua. Elizabeth Linder, Ben's mother, summed up her own feelings about her son's work. 'He had a dream', she said, 'of a Nicaragua where the day would not end for people as soon as the sun went down. He wanted to provide light after darkness for Nicaraguans to read and talk by. For that he was killed.'

The media were buzzing with the news of Ben Linder's death. Everywhere droves of reporters descended, and every word and action was recorded for international consumption. The fact that the Linder family were so articulate and helpful in the circumstances of their tragedy also helped. Some journalists were shocked by what had happened, some knew the dead man. Others were speeding around making as much money as possible while the going was good. I was slightly shocked when a reporter of my acquaintance burst upon me to announce excitedly that he had spoken to Ben Linder just two weeks before his death. It had been a low-key piece about the water project. Now he was going to syndicate the interview, which would be a world exclusive. I have to say that I found his attitude to

Linder's death quite sordid, but once again the nature of many press correspondents was visited upon me.

Then the 'investigation' began. Suggestions were being made that Linder was armed at the time of his death, that he was a member of the local milita and therefore a legitimate target. None of this was ever proven, indeed no evidence was put forward to link a gun to the dead man. While it was possible that he had participated in the militia locally, this force operated only defensively, watching out at night for Contra invasions. It was at least unlikely that Ben Linder would have been guarding the community and bending over a river at one and the same time. Yet the story was published widely in the US press. Another story, this time in *Time* magazine, cast a critical eye on the Linder family. The parents were exploiting their son's death for political reasons, went the story. It then delved into their backgrounds, and came to the conclusion that John and Elizabeth Linder had been radical Jews in their youth, non-conformist and generally critical of US foreign policy. This story suggested that the death of their son was a happy coincidence, which enabled them to put forward their radical extremist views. All of this goes to show that facts do not speak for themselves. They are interpreted and moulded by journalists, who bear a great responsibility to state things as they are. Even when editors are pushing for 'a new angle' on a story, it is dishonest to conjecture mischievously without regard to the truth.

While the international press operates with great freedom and financial wherewithal in Nicaragua, the problems of the local press are of a different nature. The big difficulty is the shortage of paper, ink and photographic film. The emphasis is on making the newspapers as widely available as possible. At 30 cordobas (at a time when the dollar was exchanging for 2,400 cordobas) *Barricada* and *Nuevo Diario* are the cheapest newspapers in Central America, and the most widely-read per head of population. They are limited to eight pages per issue because of the rationing of paper, but there is a healthy and open coverage of the situation in the space allowed. Two debates which were ongoing while I was in the country were about problems with the distribution of food to remote areas and the black market in the city, and about women's independence and rights to divorce. *La Prensa*, which had taken a very antagonistic stance to the Nicaraguan government, was banned as a direct result of the vote of 100 million dollars in Contra aid. That ban was repealed in September 1987 as part of the Central American peace plan. On my first visit to Nicaragua in July 1986, *La Prensa* was available and running some funny and unbelievable stories. One stated that chickens were being born with two heads in Nicaragua as evidence of God's anger at the Sandinista government. While recognising the demoralising effect these stories, and the more serious editorial carping of *La Prensa*, could have, I think it was a mistake to take the step of banning it.

Censorship is very rarely justified. In Nicaragua, the banning of *La Prensa* was out of keeping with the generally high level of discussion allowed in Nicaraguan society. Even the decision to ban it was argued hotly, while I was present, on several occasions in 1986. When the suppression of *La Prensa* took place, it was heralded as an example of the lack of freedom inherent in Sandinista Nicaragua by the US administration. In fact, I believe the ban was decided on from a dejected sense of helplessness, following the vote of 100 million dollars of aid to the Contras. It was a reaction, and the wrong one. As well as the political capital that was made of the censorship internationally, inside Nicaragua it led to discontent. People vociferously decried the government for cutting off an opposition outlet in this way. And the views that *La Prensa* published were still represented on radio, in the streets and in letters to other newspapers. Making it a little more difficult to get over their message was a mistake, as the government realised when they lifted the ban in 1987.

Since its re-publication, *La Prensa* has continued in its former editorial line. On 9   October 1987 they condemned Daniel Ortega's speech to the United Nations as placing too much emphasis on the 'secondary' issue of the war. They made no reference, on the other hand, to President Reagan's speech of a few days previously, to the Organisation of

American States, in which he promised to fight 'as long as there is breath in this body' to get 270 million dollars in aid for the Contras. Similarly, they pooh-poohed the surrender of arms of 400 Miskito Contras, with the charge that their leader Uriel Vanegas had been working for the Sandinistas since 1984. This was substantiated as follows: 'People who know Vanegas very well . . . declared in our editorial offices . . .' Yet even Miskito Contra leader, Steadman Fagoth, seemed to diverge from this analysis when quoted in the *Miami Herald* about Vanegas' surrender of arms. He commented, 'They don't want the war anymore'. In another editorial, *La Prensa* erroneously stated that the Nicaraguan army had 600,000 men, and was now the seventh largest army in the world. The aim of this, according to *La Prensa*, was to create a family dictatorship like that which exists in North Korea, a heavily militarised society. This was a blatant attempt to stir up antagonism to the two-year conscription which has existed for young Nicaraguan men since 1983. It is far better, of course, to allow *La Prensa* to say its worst than to ban it. Yet few countries at war allow the opposition this freedom. Even in Ireland, the government allows itself the luxury of emergency legislation and the notorious Section 31 of the Broadcasting Act, where a war is not deemed to exist.

A vibrant press exists in Nicaragua. The foreign correspondents, with their brash manners and expensive equipment, fight for space with local journalists, with much-used tapes and shortages of film. The people lap up the news and love debate, whether on the radio or television or in the columns of the newspapers. From my own experience of travel in different countries and from talking to more well-travelled journalists in Nicaragua, one difference was striking. There the poorest people, standing in a queue for the bus or at the market, would be avidly reading their daily paper. Literacy and freedom were hard fought for, and they are cherished dearly.

# The Three-Legged Stool

'Tortillas! . . . Frescos! . . . dollars?', the cries of the 'Oriental' market in downtown Managua. It's a hectic place. At the entrance are the sticky buns and sweet cakes. Then stalls full of vegetables, condiments, and brightly-coloured food dyes. (Could anyone believe the food would naturally have those shades of fuchsia, jade and orange?) Then there are alcohol stands. Bring your own bottle, because glass is in much shorter supply than drink. There's handmade leather, souvenirs of Masayan embroidery, Indian masks and the bright depictions of village life which Westerners have called 'primitive art'.

The black market is rampant in the 'Oriental'. This is where foreign film crews come to get virulently anti-government interviews. They exchange dollars at rates almost twice the official bank rate. And they sell the imported items which are currently so scarce in Managua. One day I was approached by a woman with a bucket full of cloths, or so it seemed. She smiled and lifted the cloth on top, to reveal kilos of raw fresh meat. At the best of times, the look of bloody steak makes me feel weak. On that occasion I was supposed to react with unsuppressed delight. I just nodded no, and moved on quickly. There are strict laws regulating cattle slaughter, as so many ranchers smuggled their herds out of the country, and it's a valuable export commodity.

The reason for the prevalence of the black market stems from the scarcity of many goods in Nicaragua today. Because of lack of foreign currency, imports are in short supply. Home-produced items which have an international value, like meat, are largely exported to reduce the balance of payments deficit. To discover why the economy is so squeezed we need to go back and examine the origins and operation of the economic squeeze on Nicaragua.

The economic situation inherited by the Sandinista government in 1979 was a bleak one. Gross Domestic Product, already low, had dropped by one-third over the previous two years of insurrection and conflict. Crops had not been sown by many large producers who predicted the outcome of the war. Cattle had been taken across the border in their thousands. Somoza himself had run up an external debt of 1.6 billion dollars in the previous few years, 'but there was little evidence of productive investments. The funds had been used to finance capital flight, and only 3 million dollars were left in the reserves from these loans and the bumper 1978-79 export harvest of cotton, coffee and sugar'. In addition, the 1979-80 coffee harvest had already been 'sold', though not picked, before the Sandinista Triumph.[1]

The new government had promised economic and social reform, and the provision of basic needs for the whole population. This was a tall order in terms of the legacy of inequality and poverty it had inherited. The poorest 50 per cent of Nicaraguans received 15% of national income, the richest 5% almost twice that. Two-thirds of peasant farmers had no land, or plots too small to support them. There was 20% unemployment in Managua and a huge amount of under-employment. 90% of medical services catered for only 10% of the population. One baby in eight under one year old died, and two-thirds of children under five were undernourished. 93% of rural homes had no safe drinking water, and 94% of rural children were unable to finish even primary schooling.[2]

One of the first legislative acts after July 1979 provided for nationalisation of the banks and foreign trade. The distribution of basic foodstuffs was placed under control, so that everyone was entitled to a survival amount. People with money could no longer jump the queue. Health, education and transportation were equally regarded as essentials for all, and the provision of basic health care and literacy began immediately, with the enthusiastic involvement of volunteer workers. The property of the Somoza family and their closest associates was expropriated, leading to the redistribution of 20% of the country's assets, both agricultural and industrial. Land was freed for the country's poorest peasants, who had been working for landlords up to then, often as seasonal labourers.

The economic system introduced was a largely untried one, the mixed economy. The nationalisations fitted the context of a socialist system, but private producers were given a guaranteed place in the new economic order. There were state farms, but there were also co-operatives of small-holding peasants, and 'patriotic' large producers. (These were people who had not opposed the revolutionary process, and who had continued to grow and harvest for the new economy.) There were state outlets for basic goods, but there was also an open market where people could buy luxury goods. Basic health care began to spread to the countryside and doctors were made to travel to these areas, but doctors who stayed in Nicaragua were also allowed to maintain some private practice. In state-controlled industries (such as the Victoria beer company), wages were centrally decided, but workers could join free trade unions to organise to better their individual situations.

Even in this early period, before the Contra war started to drain the economy in 1983, there were winners and losers. The President of the Association of Private Producers (COSEP), Enrique Bolanos, told me in 1986 that he had been unfairly expropriated back in 1980, although he was producing goods for the new economy. He had never been closely connected with Somoza, and yet his country home and lands had been taken from him. The government was communistic, he felt. Fr. Xavier Gorostiaga, a Jesuit working with the CIIR (Catholic Institute for International Relations), disagreed when I put this point to him. Bolanos had had hundreds of acres of land in the densely populated area of Masaya, where peasants were crying out for land. Much of his land was lying unproductive, while more was used only for grazing cattle. It had been given over to local people, who were now tilling it and providing food for the whole locality. He still owned quite a bit of land in the countryside, as well as being involved in industry. And while it was true that his country home had been confiscated, he still had a very ample home in Managua, said Fr. Gorostiaga.

Land is a key issue in Nicaragua. The country is primarily agricultural, with only a tiny industrial sector producing basic commodities for the home market. There is some mining of gold and other precious metals, but the vast majority of Nicaragua's export earnings come from agricultural goods. Coffee alone accounts for almost one half of foreign income, with cotton and sugar ranking next in importance. The country is, therefore, a hostage to fluctuations in price of these basics. The cushion of industrialisation and diversification does not exist. If a crop fails or its price declines, devastation and hunger follow. This is perhaps the classic definition of underdevelopment. Despite what has been achieved in terms of distribution of available wealth, the amount of that wealth remains small and decided by external factors.

The year after they took power the FSLN implemented their 'Emergency Economic Plan to Benefit the People'. Food production and consumption was increased, with an aim of self-sufficiency in food by 1990. 95,000 new jobs were created, and peasant co-operatives established on the land which had been expropriated from Somoza and his associates. The peasants' union carried out a big recruitment drive, concentrating on the large estates which were unorganised. A campaign for better wages and conditions followed immediately.

In July 1981 the Agrarian Reform law was introduced. In the following three years 49,661 families received titles to land[3], and about a quarter of a million people were directly affected by this improvement. Many of the resulting small and medium holdings formed themselves together into peasant co-operatives which enabled them to get credit from government agencies. They now produce three-quarters of the food for local consumption and 40% of the country's export crops.[4] Many of the large estates which were taken over after 1979 are now state farms, producing major export crops like coffee. Food and basic housing is supplied for the workers on these farms, along with the staple priorities of health, education and social support. The remaining land is in the hands of the private sector. These producers account for 50% of the land, and the government states that they are not in danger of being squeezed out; the only requirement is that they use the land in some productive way. While some of the private producers at the open meetings with government personnel complained about low prices for their produce and poor transportation and distribution, they did not seem under threat as a category of producers. The commitment to a mixed economy is real.

Agrarian reform is continuing. Figures available for 1979-1986 show that a total of 97,000 families (600,000 people) have received land totalling nearly 2 million hectares. This equals 31% of the cultivable land in the country, and half of the rural population have directly gained from the agrarian reform.[5] These direct gains from the overthrow of the oligarchy are obvious in the Nicaraguan countryside. They make the peasantry the staunchest supporters of the new government and, by the accounts of development workers, the people whose circumstances have leapt forward most in the past ten years.

I picked coffee on one of the state-run farms over Christmas 1986, and the start of 1987. These farms account for a million hectares of land, making the total amount of land included in the reforms equal to 3 million hectares. When we arrived at the farm we were greeted by one of the local supervisors, who told us how important international helpers were because so many local pickers were away at the war front. He apologised in advance for the food we would have to put up with for the next four weeks. It would be rice and beans, with tortillas (a kind of corn pancake), which was what the local farmers survived on all year. There was no extra money to provide 'goodies' for international helpers. We all nodded, no problem, that was as it should be, and piled into the back of a lorry to go the last few miles to the house we'd be staying in. Every bone was shaken as we stood upright in the back of the lorry. At first we kept saying 'sorry' to each other as we were thrown around. Then we gave that up and concentrated on survival.

We were one of the luckiest of the international brigades, because the house we drew up in front of was an old hacienda, which had belonged to one of Somoza's generals before 1979. It was big and imposing, if a bit run down, but we were thrilled to hear we had an inside toilet and shower. The house was like something out of *Gone with the Wind*, with a big porch overlooking the surrounding countryside, and bushes of bright purple and red bougainvillaea. There was a row of palm trees along what must have been 'the drive', and children played in the dried-up ornamental pond. Inside the house we were shown our quarters, which consisted of the main reception hall and what was the General's bedroom. There were three Nicaraguan families living in the other rooms. I remember being hit by panic as I scanned the room for a good place to park my sleeping bag. I wanted a good space, because it would be 'home' for the next month. Near the toilet might be handy during the night, but maybe there'd be more risk of getting sick there. One end of the room had no light, but it was quieter. The General's bedroom was beside the kitchen, which I rightly surmised would be hot and noisy in the mornings. In the end I just threw my sleeping bag down in the middle of the room, where there was lots of light to read by, but perhaps too much traffic.

There were thirty people on the brigade, twenty-six English, three Irish and one Australian. Sleeping beside me on the floor was Siobhan, an Australian of Irish descent. She started joking about becoming an honorary member of the 'Irish Brigade' since she was convinced that's where the 'crack' would be after witnessing our first night in Managua. Beside her was Graham with 'The urge for destruction can also be a creative urge — Bakunin' written on his t-shirt. He was a strict vegetarian, and later on when we found a poisonous snake in the coffee bushes he opposed killing it. 'It was here first', he said. That didn't stop us shouting for one of the locals, who beheaded the snake with one blow of his 'machete' (an implement like a straight sickle). What a relief! Opposite me on the ground was Eddie, an Irish trade union

65

official. He was an old hand at brigades of every sort, and immediately began cracking jokes and unpacking song books. That would be great. Loads of sad Irish dirges.

On our first day, there was a meeting (not the first of many, I hoped). One of the Englishwomen approached me to say there had been quite a debate at the planning meeting in London about what to call the brigade. It had been agreed that, since women are the unwritten rebels of history, the brigade should be called after a woman. Angela, who was telling me about this, said that she had proposed that the brigade be called after the two Irish women prisoners in Britain, Martina Anderson and Ella O'Dwyer. After a lot of debate this had been voted down on the basis that none of the Irish people were present, and it would be important what we thought. I thought this was a bit of a cop-out, since the issue involved was the strip-searching of prisoners in English jails, an issue English people should have their own views on. At the meeting, the women who had felt badly about the earlier vote proposed that at a minimum a letter of support should be sent to the Irishwomen, and a note criticising such punitive practices should be sent to the British Home Secretary, pointing to the example of the rehabilitative prison system in Nicaragua. That was passed unanimously. It was then decided that we could use our presence to get some publicity for the largely forgotten women of GAM in Guatemala. GAM stands for Grupo Apoyo Mutuo (Mutual Support Group), and it consists of relatives of people who have been 'disappeared' by the Guatemalan Army. (This region coined this use of the verb disappear. People don't disappear, they *are* disappeared). Thousands of Guatemalans have becme refugees, others are killed openly in the streets and villages to spread a lesson of fear among the population. The Mutual Support Group is the only opposition operating in Guatemala itself. Although they are under constant threat of being killed themselves, they publicise the cases of disappeared people, often using international supporters as company and cover for their own protection. Rosario Cuevas was a member of GAM and a mother of two children when she was killed by the military just over three years ago. We became the Rosario

Cuevas Brigade.

We were all in pretty good spirits as we settled in for that first night on the tile floor. I was tired and hung over from the previous night's celebratory introductions, so I knew I'd sleep standing up. After what seemed like moments, I was awake again. It was pitch dark, but in the distance a radio was playing the rousing anthem, the Himno del Frente Sandinista. I dragged myself up slowly, threw some water on my face and got into the queue for breakfast. It was ten past five as I came face to face with the first morning plate of beans and rice. It went down pretty heavily. I could see straight away that there were certain people I would have to avoid in the mornings. One was a really bright chirpy woman who had adopted a cheerleader stance, and was jollying everyone along. I just wanted to take it easy and quiet. By five forty-five we had our mountain boots on and we started the long trek up the coffee slopes. The sun was just peeking up over the lush velvet green mountains. It was extremely beautiful, and very calming, but it was damn tiring. The coffee fields were high up, and it was a struggle getting there. A combination of breathlessness and the burning pain of exertion are something to feel at six o'clock in the morning. Ahead of me Nicaraguan children bounded along, energetic and eager to get at it.

When we arrived at our coffee field we got a lesson in bean harvesting. The red beans were called rojitas, and they looked juicy and ready to be picked. There were green beans that looked distinctly unhealthy, which you wouldn't look at. In between there were red and yellow berries, which were ok to harvest, and red and green ones which were to be left behind. These last are called 'pintos', and sometimes a bean would look red but when you picked it there was green underneath! Horror of horrors! These pintos had to be kept separately, where they could be used for the making of lower quality non-export coffee. We put our heads down and started to pick. Harvesting the beans was quite easy really; after a while you could tell by the feel of a berry whether it was ready to come away from the tree. You dropped the beans into a basket tied around your waist. When the basket was full you popped the beans into your sack and moved methodically along your own row.

There weren't many problems once you got in on the picking routine. When it was raining, though, the slopes would be really slippy with the mud giving way suddenly under your feet. Not only had you to try to stay upright, but you had to make sure you didn't spill any beans while you were at it. At times you would have to tie yourself to a coffee bush to keep upright. Some bushes were so small you'd have to lie under them to get at the berries. Others were so tall that you'd have to tie them down with ropes before you could even start picking. Both of these operations were back-breaking. Then there were the insects, mainly hornets and caterpillars. The caterpillars were luminous green and very hairy. They were about a foot long, and if you put your hand on one without looking it administered a poison that paralysed your arm for about an hour. We were lucky; this only happened once to one of the group. Then there were the snakes, which we westerners have a real phobia about maybe because of the serpent in Paradise. We spent days anticipating seeing a snake and wondering what we'd do.

When a snake did finally show up he was lying fast asleep on a branch of a coffee bush. He was small, about two foot long and thin, with black and white markings. One of the Nicaraguans with us told us that this snake was indeed poisonous and he knocked it to the ground before killing it quickly with his machete. It was a baby snake, he told us. The bizarre thing was that the next day we found a similar snake in size and markings in the exact same bush. It too was quickly dispatched. It was obviously a nest and I began to think that if these were the two baby snakes in the nest, surely the mother was not going to allow us away with killing off her progeny. I had visions, like a bad horror movie, of this huge snake suddenly appearing over the top of the bush and killing us all to avenge her loss! But this didn't happen, and we didn't see any more snakes during our time coffee-picking.

The rows were planted close together, which was great, because it meant you were within earshot of eight or ten people. This was of great importance when you had ten hours to spend doing such mentally undemanding work.

Conversations would start up on housing co-operatives in London, on why your last relationship broke up or on favourite films and stage shows. Other days were spent playing 'Botticelli' and other forms of Who's Who. But my favourite time-passer was an English actor called Jonathan, who as a child had loved military history. At the merest suggestion of 'Waterloo' or 'Culloden' he would launch into a theatrical description of the battle strategies, the personalities of the generals and the outcome and effects of the fight on history. This was riveting. Even Janet, from CND, reluctantly had to admit it was good stuff.

It's extraordinary to see what a bit of hardship can do to people. Normally polite folk would get thoroughly engrossed in discussions on each other's bowel problems. Most people suffered from dysentery and diarrhoea at some stage. The fear of it, and its truly sickening nature when it struck, were enough to engross most of us in the subject. At one stage, dengue fever struck some of the brigade. It was a real tropical nightmare, involving delusions, massive weight loss and high temperature. It lasted about four days, and during that time the people affected looked at death's door. But they recovered when the fever waned, and no one got an illness that would damage them in the long term.

The day's work ended at four o'clock, and we took turns at going to the weighing session afterwards. The beans we collected would be weighed, as would those of our Nicaraguan colleagues. The comparison between what they could pick and what we had managed was embarrassing. But it was a nice part of the day, winding down after the hard slog, with a shower and dinner beckoning. The evenings went very fast. Once we had eaten, the sun had gone down and it was totally dark outside. It was dangerous to venture out in the darkness, because of snakes or the possibility of falling. In addition the Contras had named coffee-pickers as economic targets, and there was a risk they would snatch any stray pickers found wandering in the dark. So we stayed indoors at night. It wasn't too hard to fill those couple of hours before sleep — a small chat, a sing-song, a game of cards or chess, a read, and zonk, you were asleep without noticing yourself going.

We picked coffee for four weeks and at the end of that time we were very tired. The monotony of the diet was hard to put up with. By the end of the second week some people wouldn't face the beans and rice. Others just about managed to stomach it with the addition of little bits of spices and tomato puree that they'd brought with them. But for the Nicaraguans who work the coffee-harvest for the three harvesting months of the year, these conditions are their regular life. And they know the importance of their work to the survival of the Nicaraguan economy. While we were working in Matagalpa, we attended some union meetings. There the coffee harvesters would discuss this year's harvest, the price of coffee worldwide and how the output of that region was vital to the country's economy. They knew that Nicaragua's survival was bound up with the improvements that have been made in the last few years, and they didn't want to go back. As well as the basic improvements in food supplies, nurseries, maternity and sick leave and adult education, there was one other change from the old days. Every Saturday night, the UPE or state farm provided the rum for a party which was held in the old General's hacienda. There was music and dancing after the hard week. As I sat one night on the porch of the house while one of these parties was in progress, a local woman told us that in Somoza's day that porch would be full of Guardia, of whom the locals were terrified. If a woman went out after dark, she was likely to be set upon and raped by these thugs, she said. Now things were different. The house was used by local families, international helpers, and the community as a whole. It had been appropriated by the people for their use and enjoyment.

In 1985-6 Nicaragua produced 665,000 quintals of coffee (one quintal = 100 lbs.) Higher prices for coffee had materialised because of a drought in Brazil, the country that supplies most of the world's coffee. Prices went up from 150 dollars per quintal to 267 dollars.[6] The result was an increase in foreign exchange from coffee for that year of 60 million dollars. This was also due to the participation once again of parts of Northern Jinotega and Matagalpa in the coffee harvest, which had been abandoned for a few years because of Contra activity. Every dollar earned from coffee exports plays a vital role in economic development, stability, and in Nicaragua's ability to buy goods abroad to raise its living standards. Unfortunately, increasing amounts of dollars also go to the war, and last year fifty per cent of the country's budget was spent on defence and the replacement of goods and facilities lost as a direct result of the war. In March 1987, production losses caused by the war equalled 503 million dollars, which is equal to forty per cent of all export earnings in the five years of war.[7] The cost of arms and defence is huge for any country at war. For a country as poor as Nicaragua, the results are immediate and devastating.

The Contra war has been well chronicled, and its disastrous effects are known internationally. What is not so well known is the war waged on another level — the economic embargo. The charge that the resistance to the Nicaraguan government comes from Nicaraguans themselves does not stick when we turn our attention from the military war to the economic war. Here the fight goes on at boardroom level in Washington and New York. And the fighters, wearing suits rather than khaki, are bankers, business people and politicians.

Every third world country depends on aid and loans from the developed world to survive. The money that was taken in colonial times in the form of raw materials allowed the development of the Western economies. Now that development makes them rich enough to lend money to their poorer neighbours, at a rate of interest. An important power like the United States can cause huge suffering by using its economic weight to try to change a country's political system. This is what Ronald Reagan's administration has done since coming to power in 1980.

The first thing to be hit was a 10 million dollar 'Food for Peace' programme initiated by President Jimmy Carter. This was an agreement to supply wheat to Nicaragua. In March and April of 1981, the remainder of a 75 million dollar loan initiated under Carter was also cancelled. As well as the cancellation of aid and loans directly from the United States, the influence of that power over multilateral institutions was soon to bear fruit. And the pressure applied was crass and open. Lee H. Hamilton, Chairman of the House Permanent Intelligence Committee, told the *Washington Post* on 23rd March, 1985 that the US could 'increase economic pressure on Nicaragua (by) working with our allies to deny it World Bank loans and assistance from the International Monetary Fund. A policy of increased economic pressure could also include a trade cut-off.' Both of these have since come to pass.

In 1984, for the first time, no loans were allowed for Nicaragua from the International Development Bank, making it the only Latin American country to be so excluded. As well as using its veto, the US administration directly threatened to withhold moneys from the IDB if certain loans for Nicaragua were considered. Such pressure was applied to a loan application for 58 million dollars, which was to be used by small and medium scale private farmers for cultivation and housing, and for the purchase of farm machinery. In a letter dated 30 January, 1985, to the President of the IDB, Secretary of State George Schultz expressed 'strong concern' over this loan prospect. He stated the administration's disapproval of Nicaragua's economic and political policies, warning that if the loan were approved, it would make it more difficult to gain Congressional appropriations for the bank.

The World Bank also changed its view on funding for Nicaragua. In October 1981 the Bank's report: 'Nicaragua; The Challenge of Reconstruction', asserted that with financial backing 'Nicaragua will indeed be able to enhance the social situation of its citizens'. In that year, only the US voted against aid. By the next year, though, there had been a change of heart. The 1982 Country Program Paper of the World Bank urged a stop to loans until such time as Nicaragua would agree with policy recommendations from the Bank. Since 1982 Nicaragua has not received any World Bank funding.[8]

The result of the cuts in aid and favourable loans from the large multilateral agencies, from 78% in 1979 to 2.8% in 1986, is that the loans provided now are tied to shorter pay-back periods, to purchases of specific goods or to bilateral trade agreements. Nicaragua has less freedom in how it spends the dollars borrowed, and the economy is burdened with unattractive interest payments. In 1986, nearly 90 million dollars went on servicing of debt alone, and cash available for freely chosen imports dropped from 37% to 25% between 1985 and 1986.[9]

This high-level attempt to isolate Nicaragua has had huge effects on how people live. But it has not completely succeeded. Direct aid continues, mainly emanating from the European Community and the Socialist Bloc. The Social Democratic governments of Western Europe (in particular France and Spain) vigorously opposed suggestions of a cut-off of EC aid and trade. In 1984 Nicaragua remained the main beneficiary of EC food aid in Central America, receiving 9.11 million ECUs (i.e. The European Currency Unit, which equals 83 U.S. cents). They also received 330,000 ECUs towards aiding displaced persons in that year. While the discussion of EC aid is ongoing, with Britain taking the US 'no aid' line, so far Nicaragua has not been isolated from European support. In fact, Eurocrats have been known to point to Central America as a case demonstrating Europe's independence in foreign policy issues. What has been done is small, but the aid and what it represents is crucial.

I was very pleased to get to talk to one of Nicaragua's foremost economic thinkers while I was there. Xavier Gorostiaga is a Jesuit involved with Nicaragua's Ministry of Economic Planning. I joined a briefing he was giving to students of the Kellogg Foundation in his office in Managua. (They are a group of people who are travelling the world on this strange scholarship, which allows the group to travel to each country nominated by any one of them. They happened to be in Nicaragua because one individual wanted to examine the music of the Atlantic Coast area.) Xavier Gorostiaga was an enthusiast for his subject, and happily fielded the occasionally naïve questions put to him. Nicaragua wanted a diverse aid and trade pattern. It was like having a stool with four legs, he said. The United States was one leg, Western Europe, the socialist countries and the non-aligned nations were the other three legs. Reflecting the mixed economy at home, Nicaragua desired to have dealings with all four sectors of the world economy. The trade embargo imposed by the United States in 1985 had knocked away one of those four legs. But the government was determined, he said, not to be made solely dependent on trade with the Soviet/socialist bloc. While the economy has been pushed in that direction, it is busily seeking out new and diverse markets for its produce. The Sandinista government never tried to lose its trade with the US, and in fact US imports accounted for 26% of total imports in 1981, only 3% less than in 1977.

Between 1980 and 1984 Nicaraguan trade with Western Europe, for example, increased from 235 million dollars to 308 million dollars. Imports from Europe doubled in that period from 87.8 m. dollars to 169.4 m. dollars, while exports fell slightly from 147.7 m. dollars to 138.8 m. dollars[10]. (Figures from the Nicaraguan Ministry of External Co-operation). However, the need to pay hard cash for imports from most countries has reduced Nicaragua's ability to trade widely. Up to 1982 it was buying most of its oil from Venezuela and Mexico. But in 1983, because it was falling behind on payments, the oil shipments started to fall off. Now, over 80% of the country's oil needs are provided by the Soviet Union, on very favourable terms. In this way, the squeezing of credit and the cut-off of trade with the United States has driven Nicaragua into closer economic ties with the Socialist Bloc. In 1982 the industrialised western countries were still responsible for 32% of loans and aid, the socialist countries for 19% and other third world countries for 49%. But by 1984 the share of foreign loans from socialist countries had risen to 60 per cent. There is an element of the self-fulfilling prophecy in the United States' claims that Nicaragua is a Soviet satellite. By cutting off its ability to trade with the US and by pushing its allies in Europe to follow suit, it hopes to be able to point to a total dependence on the Soviet bloc, and then say 'I told you so — Soviet economic puppets'. But this has not happened yet. The four-legged stool has become a three-legged one, but as we know from the Irish milking parlour three legs can give solid support!

Xavier Gorostiaga told me a story which I thought was indicative of the attitude of Nicaraguan traders and business people. The day the US trade embargo was announced, a boat carrying bananas sat ready to sail from Bluefields on the Atlantic Coast to the United States. When the news broke about the embargo on trade the entrepreneurial captain switched maps, changed course and at once set sail for Amsterdam. Holland became a major purchaser of Nicaraguan bananas, and Europe became a major substitute market for this product.

Coffee, which accounts for over one-third of Nicaragua's export revenue, is now sold mainly to Western Europe, particularly West Germany and the Netherlands. Japan and Taiwan buy most of the cotton, and sugar is sold to Mexico, Algeria and the Soviet Union.[11] But diversification is only part of the solution, and Nicaragua's external economic sector is in a very bad way. While imports have remained fairly constant since 1980, at between 800 and 900 million dollars, the volume and terms of trade have devalued the income from exports from 508 million dollars in 1981 to only 218 million dollars in 1986. This has fuelled a galloping inflation rate at home, and has inflated the value of the dollar, leading to the creation of a dollar black market.[12] There was a negative growth-rate of the order of 5 and 6% in 1985 and 1986, and in inflation neared 700% in 1986. By 1987 inflation had reached 1500%. These economic indicators, while alarming, must be put in the context of other Latin American countries, where inflation can be 2,000 to 3,000%. But the steady decline in Nicaragua's economic fortunes can be almost totally put down to the war on two fronts, the economic and the military. The economic costs of the Contra war are estimated at 2,821 million dollars, more than the total annual national budget (2,428 million dollars). And a large number of the country's youth are caught up in defence, at a time when they would be at their most useful economically. The old and the weak are left to do the farming along with the women.

The internal economy too has been shaken. The government tried to boost production in industry and agriculture, recognising that only a real increase in output would stabilise the economy's base. In agriculture, there has been an increase in productivity in the war-free areas, mainly due to a new pricing policy which allows individual peasants and co-operatives to gain financially from increased sales of produce. In the cities, a system of cards enabled workers in direct production to buy goods at low prices in special supermarkets. This seemed an attractive subsidy to urban producers. However, pressure for these cards increased the number in circulation from 100,000 in 1983 to 350,000 in 1986[13]. They were no longer a stimulus to production, merely a help to the urban poor.

At the same time there is a constant demand for imported products. The 'Buhoneros' who travel abroad and sell such commodities have been bleeding the domestic economy with their constant demand for dollars to buy goods abroad. It is understandable that a country that has seen such hardship and repression in the past should now want some of the fruits of a better life. But what is happening is that a black market has been established, giving advantages to people with access to dollars (from relatives abroad, for example), and draining any wealth that does exist out of the country. This creates a downward economic spiral.

As in other areas, the reflex of the Nicaraguan government has been to allow maximum freedom, while providing for the basics of life, basic food, health, housing and education. They have allowed the black market to continue to exist rather than suppress it. It allows an outlet for people with more money to buy their meat and foreign soaps, rather than insisting on adherence to local produce alone. This has led to considerable debate, especially from international workers, who feel that the black marketeers should be simply arrested, and the operation of the black market stopped. The government instead is trying the art of persuasion rather than repression. The state itself has opened a dollar shop in Managua, where people can buy the tinned meats and biscuits that scarcity makes so attractive. I remember going in there myself and feeling my heart racing at the sight of cheddar cheese and butter. The shop seems to work. It has a turnover of 6 million dollars per annum, of which 1 million dollars is profit. This money then goes into the state coffers and is used to subvent social programmes, and to help with the external deficit. It's another example of the mixed economy at work.

One day I spotted an unusual demonstration organised by the Sandinista Youth. It was made up of about two dozen floats on which young people dressed in stark and varied costumes depicted the different aspects of the black market. The short plays showed how the black marketeers were running down the country by sending dollars abroad illegally in exchange for luxury goods. The message was that this effort should instead go into providing a proper life for everyone. It was delivered with plenty of singing and dancing, and much jumping off floats to involve passers-by in the spectacle.

The Nicaraguan economic system has its critics on both the right and the left. The US administration and its allies point to the confiscations of land, the limitations on owner-ship of wealth, the interference with the free operation of the market. They point to the fact that professionals such as doctors have to spend part of their week working in state hospitals or travelling to rural health clinics. They criticise the lack of freedom inherent in the insistence on agricultural productivity: a person is no longer free to leave land idle for periods. On the left, critics of Nicaragua point to the existence of a market determining supply and demand rather than a centrally-controlled distribution system, the continued differences in personal wealth, and the non-suppression of the black market in goods and dollars. They point to the continued ability of some Nicaraguans to travel abroad, and the non-confiscation of many big houses in Managua.

Both sets of critics point to real inadequacies from their points of view. But the new Nicaraguan state promised only one thing to its citizens back in 1979 — the basic social wage of adequate nutrition, housing for all and the improvement of social services. They have genuinely achieved that base, despite setbacks caused by the weight of defence expenditure. Unlike other Central and Latin American states, there is a real effort to prevent children going to bed hungry in Nicaragua, and every family has a roof over its head. There are real hardships and scarcities of goods, but the current redistribution, while leaving some quite well off, has ensured that now everyone is at least on the first rung of the ladder above survival level.

The shortages and the struggle to overcome adversity were brought home to me one day when I went to visit a project in the Sebaco valley in western Nicaragua. It was funded by the Irish development agency, Trocaire, and Fermin, a Chilean who used to live in Ireland, was working there. It was an agricultural school, with a difference. The students, many of them experienced farmers, were learning not only how to drive tractors and use agricultural machinery, but how to repair and reconstruct these valuable tools when they broke down. Because of the trade embargo imposed by the US, spare parts for machinery are very hard to come by. On the floor of one of the buildings lay thousands of nuts, bolts and small repair parts which obviously meant something to the students there, but which to me just looked like stacks of useless spare pieces from different tractor models. The students take broken-down machinery, find the spare part that most closely resembles the broken item, and modify it to fit. Hundreds of dysfunctional agricultural machines have been made to work again in this school, and the students I met were excited at the prospect of helping their country's agriculture to modernise. Positive discrimination is applied to encourage women, who have tended to be ignored in farming families, to learn these vital skills. While the first women who came to study were ridiculed by their colleagues, Fermin told me, now they make up nearly half the number and are integrated completely.

The school is set in a beautiful part of the country, a valley surrounded on all sides by picturesque mountains. The house has beautiful verandahs all around it to take full advantage of the view. The garden in proximity to the house is full of cultivated and rare fruit trees, peach, mandarin, oranges, wine apples. They date from the time when the house was owned by an absentee landlord, who spent most of his time in Florida. The house and lands were confiscated in 1980 and put to this productive use. The school supports itself and its students from the products of the farm, selling them in the local market. Fermin told me that when he first went to work there an old woman who lived locally told him that all of that land (about 200 acres) had been sealed off and private. No one had seen the owner for years, but his rule was enforced and people were not even allowed to traverse the land. The woman said that a great mystique had grown up about the 'patron', as well as a dislike of him, because people's lives were made very difficult by this land being totally closed. Now the students are esconced in the big house, and they hold 'open days' and fiestas to which all the local people are welcome. On the day I visited, lunch of fish and rice was served in a straw-roofed kitchen, open to the air of the valley. The talk was rapid and enthusiastic. The tiny fish were delicious, and I fully understood why everyone else seemed to be gobbling them up, heads and all. It was the first fish they had had in two months, by coincidence, and the break from vegetables was well appreciated.

Yet even here danger lurks. The surrounding hills contain some Contra camps, and this school has been declared an economic target. At night, after teaching and tilling, cooking and repairing all day, the staff and students must take their turns at militia duty, keeping a watch for attacks. So far this has been successful. There have been a number of forays, but no one has been killed and nothing substantial destroyed. 'But', says Fermin, 'it's so hard keeping a watch, trying to stay awake all night. And of course, the mosquitoes are eating you alive.' I thought that day as I left Sebaco that so much productive economic effort is being dissipated and wasted on merely preventing disaster, but it seems that such defensive measures will continue to sap Nicaraguan energy for some time to come.

1. E.V.K. Fitzgerald, *Stabilisation and Economic Justice: the Case of Nicaragua*, Kellogg Institute for International Studies, Notre Dame, Paper 34, Sept. 1984, p. 13.
2. Quoted in Melrose, *Nicaragua, The Threat of a Good Example*.
3. 'Agrarian Reform: Summary of Titles Given', CIERA, 1984.
4. *Envio*, July 1984.

5. Annual Information Bulletin No. 48, 22nd Nov. 1986, p. 11. Quoted in *Here Nobody Surrenders*.
6. *Update,* Central American Historical Institute bulletin, No. 14, 27th May, 1987. Available through the Catholic Institute for International Relations (CIIR), 22 Coleman Fields, London NI 7AF.
7. *Update,* No. 20, 20th July, 1987.
8. *Update,* Vol. 4, No. 9, 1st April, 1985, p. 3.
9. *Update,* No. 20, 20th July, 1987.
10. *The Philosophy and Politics of the Government of Nicaragua,* March 1982.
11. *Update,* No. 46, 31st Jan., 1985.
12. *Envio,* No. 73, July 1987.
13. *Envio,* Vol. 5, No. 63, Sept. 1986, 'Slow motion towards a survival economy'.

# Getting in Control

José played the guitar and worked in the telephone company. He was taking maths exams at night, and hoped to become a skilled telephone technician. He invited me to call by his house in Managua one night, and I found it among the wooden shanties of the city. I received a warm unhurried reception from José's parents and his grandmother, who wanted me to take her rocking chair, the best seat in the house. When I said no, I was fine on a stool, she was amused. I was given a large mug of Nicaragua's national beverage, a juice made from ground corn, and I had to concentrate quite hard not to wince as it slipped down. An acquired taste, definitely.

José's father worked at the Victoria beer company and had done all his life. It was a good job, he said, he had to fish out dead rats from the vats of beer. He watched my reaction. I said that we had many people employed doing the same in our beer factories at home. He had a good laugh at this. They had a social club in the firm, and on Saturdays he and his wife would go there. The drink was cheap and the dancing good.

The family had lived in a brick house up until the earthquake. Now their home consisted of one large room constructed of wooden slats fitted together horizontally. He showed me how this was done, remarking that I'd be the only Irishwoman who could build her own house when I got home. The room itself was divided by a piece of corrugated iron, and when I finally convinced Jose's mother to sit down, she explained that this allowed for the boys and girls to sleep separately. In the corner hung a curtain, like a make-shift dressingroom, and here all the members of the family took their turns to dress, undress and change.

Even in the quiet of the evening the house was hot. José's mother explained that this was because the roof was of corrugated iron. 'In the daytime it becomes like an oven in here', she said. 'The roof traps all the heat and makes it worse. You just have to get outside during the midday sun. I hope we can afford to get clay tiles for the roof soon, because they keep a house cool.' The floor was of the same scorched red clay as the ground outside, and she said it had to be swept five or six times every day just to keep pushing the dust outside.

While we chatted away, José finished off his maths for the evening, managing somehow to ignore the conversation and the play of the younger children at his feet. Altogether, eleven people lived in this small house, eight children, parents and grandmother. The smaller children slept on rush mats, the teenagers in hammocks. Hammocks are the simplest natural way to keep cool at night, without benefit of an electric fan or air-conditioning. The slight rocking of the hammock creates a breeze which makes the heat bearable.

It is important not to romanticise poverty and overcrowding. People make the best of the crushed situations they have to live in. The Nicaraguan personality tends to be easy-going, without our neurosis about space and privacy, though this may have developed out of necessity. From visiting many families in Nicaragua, I was surprised at how people managed to get on and concentrate on their own particular lives without feeling cramped by the proximity of their physical circumstances. That night, before we left the house to go for a drink, José and his young brother played a few tunes for the rest of the family. And then we went, leaving behind an atmosphere of easy smiles.

The families living in the city centre shanties were among the poorest in Managua. Built along the seam of the earthquake, shanties huddled together. Dogs and chickens ran in and out of the houses, which had no doors. But they were in the city centre, where people wished to remain. There has been a house-building programme in operation since 1980, and little by little the worst shanties are being replaced with brick housing. Many of these can be seen in the working class barrios just a few miles from the city centre. Here, families have running water, and four to five rooms. There are gardens in which to grow the tumbling foliage of the tropics, or vegetables like peppers, onions and marrow.

Campesino (peasant) houses have improved in the last decade. Many of them have the tiled roofs of red clay referred to by José's mother. These tiles deflect the sun's rays and are a huge advantage in living with the tropical sun. Rene, a friend I worked with while coffee picking, told me that the two biggest improvements in his life since the Sandinista revolution had been getting a tiled roof, and getting a radio! While this seemed a very frivolous bonus to me, he pointed out that you never felt cut off when you had a radio. You could hear people's views on everything. And of course, music on the radio breaks the silence of the quiet country nights, he said. I remembered then that it was not all that long ago that people gathered around a radio to hear a play or football match in Ireland. Television seems to have been with us for years, but the length of time involved is quite short.

The staple diet of the Nicaraguan people is beans and rice. The red kidney beans and white rice can be boiled separately, or fried together. Sometimes, the beans are puréed and served with fried savoury bananas. Tortillas, or corn pancakes, are the other basic food. They are very dry and endlessly chewable, with little taste. (On an earlier trip to El Salvador, I was amazed to find a group of Salvadorean refugees living in a church in San Salvador, who had lived for four years inside the building on tortillas alone.) Whatever about that diet, the rice and beans one is a perfect balance for survival, containing the right amount of protein, carbohydrates and vitamins to live on. It was suggested to me that the Somozas introduced this diet to allow them to feed large numbers of farm labourers with minimal problems. Since 1979 there have been attempts to widen and vary the Nicaraguan diet, but beans and rice remain the firm favourite.

In the 1980/1982 period, per capita consumption of the majority of basic foods increased (tables are published by the Agrarian Reform Research and Study Centre, CIERA, in Nicaragua). Beef and milk have become hard to find, because many of the larger beef ranchers took their cattle, about 200,000 head, across the border after 1979. There has been a crisis in cattle production, and people who were able to get meat under Somoza's rule, once they could pay for it, will now bitterly complain of this shortage. On the other hand, products like cooking oil, chicken, pork, eggs and sugar are now more available to the wider population than previously. Government distribution centres ensure the equitable division of these products, and the rural poor now have access to a wider diet. In some ways, the gains of the poorest campesinos have been the losses of the urban middle class, and Nicaragua's revolution has been described as a peasant revolution. The campesinos have received titles for their holdings, financial support for the establishment of co-operatives, machinery contributed from abroad and a larger portion of their produce for their own consumption. Pork too has become an important agricultural commodity. As early as 1982, the new state farms had succeeded in producing 15,000 pounds of pork each day. But this nutritional improvement has been placed in jeopardy because of Contra attacks on pork farms, which are targetted. Production vacillates from year to year.

Fruit is very plentiful in Nicaragua but, surprisingly, people are not too bothered by it. It is sold in liquid form as cool drinks by vendors at the side of the road. But the 'gaseosas' or fizzy drinks are much more popular. Sometimes Coca Cola is available, other times the carbonated drinks are two sickly sweet pink and purple versions of liquid bubble gum.

Beer is a very popular beverage, particularly among Nicaraguan men. Increasingly you will find younger women drink beer among themselves or with male 'companeros'. This would not have been possible 15 or 20 years ago, in Nicaragua's macho society, but things are slowly changing. Rum is almost always available, even when beer is not, and is very cheap. A bottle of good rum costs the equivalent of half a dollar. Scarcity and expense only arise if you insist on a mixer with the rum; this can be dearer than the drink itself or simply unavailable. Nicaraguans most commonly drink rum neat, with just a slice of lime, and drinking houses in the late evening are noisy places with singing, arguing and mariachi music all raising the sound level. Where arguments start outside the pub, the police seem to take a very lenient attitude, quietly pressing people in a homeward direction.

A fiesta is a great occasion in a country town. Here is an excuse for the whole family, old and young, men and women, to get out together and relax. Often there's a circus for the kids, a carnival for everyone, and a brass band in the main street. The sophisticated veneer of Western adults is unknown, and Nicaraguans will uninhibitedly whoop their delight on bumpers, waltzers, and big wheels. Marquees selling beer and ice cream fill up with chatting people. Very often a statue at the head of a procession will be the sole reminder that the occasion has religious connotations. One such festival I attended in Diriamba, just south of Managua, started with the procession, then a race of oxen pulling ploughs and finally, dancing and drinking until the sun peeked up and caught us.

Apart from such carousing nights, cinema is a popular form of recreation. It is interesting to note the films on offer, because the US trade embargo hits most Hollywood films. Only where the director or film company makes a definite decision will a modern film reach Nicaragua. Examples while I was there were 'The Cotton Club' and 'Latino'. Otherwise there is an insatiable interest in even the oldest movies, an interest I also developed. Speckled black and whites like 'Moses', with a very young Burt Lancaster, attracted full houses night after night. Outside, street vendors sell precious chocolate and chewing gum. A tiny bar of Chinese chocolate costs the equivalent of a dollar, so it's a luxury commodity indeed.

Children's parties are great occasions for everyone. No Nicaraguan family will scrimp on these important nights, and adult neighbours and friends come along to join the festivities. The favourite game is the Piñata — an animal made of crepe paper and filled with sweets and small toys. It hangs from a string which is manipulated on a pulley by one of the adults. The children are blindfolded and hit at the Piñata with a long stick, when the music stops. Sometimes it swings out of reach, other times they hit the target to the excitement of the onlookers. Eventually the paper gives, and the sweets tumble out, while the children scamper around the floor to gather them.

One children's party that I attended in one of the poorest barrios of Managua was typical. On the walls were two large reproductions, one of da Vinci's Last Supper and one of Che Guevara. The poor children playing at the centre of the room were all dressed exquisitely, layers of frills and flounces on the girls and brightly coloured shirts and pants on the boys. A close look revealed some careful needlework to preserve these 'best' clothes, but the overall appearance was one of party finery and ebullient fun. The proud smiles of the parents revealed another cultural difference. Where an Irish party centres on adult conversation and getting the children up to bed, or away, for Nicaraguans the best party of all is to celebrate a child's birthday or first communion. The adults chat in the background while getting the greatest kick from the laughter and satisfaction of happy children.

Incongruous as it may seem, Nicaragua's national sport is baseball. Up and down the country children play it in every field or piece of wasteland, using whatever is available to approximate to a baseball glove. There is a huge stadium in Managua where the biggest matches take place. The arc lights over it are empty of bulbs, though; it would be an extravagance to light them. Instead, the big games are held in daylight and people make elaborate arrangements to be free to go to them. When I was news reporting, we were told that the President was going to be along at one important baseball game, if we wanted to be there. Many of us didn't bother, on the basis that he would probably make some unimportant congratulatory remarks to the team. In the event, he used the occasion to air a major policy statement on defence. He joked that he knew he would get an audience at the stadium.

There is a baseball pitch situated right in the centre of Managua, which is often lit up at night. It is used by the war disabled. It is quite tragic to stand and watch thirty young men, in their best years and in such good spirits, attempting to continue living life fully despite the handicap of being confined to a wheelchair. Everything that happens in Nicaragua is affected by the fact of the Contra war.

The achievements in promoting literacy since 1979 make even the most tired and war-weary Nicaraguans proud. Marisol was a coffee worker in Matagalpa. 'Our children have a new power now, they will never be tricked or manipulated, as long as they can read. When Somoza was in charge we were paid by the number of "latas" of beans we collected,' she told me. 'But because we were illiterate and innumerate we did not know at the end of the week what our daily amounts added up to. We were often left short in our pay. In those days, too, men were able to collect the wages of their compañeras. They could head off to spend the money on alcohol while we were powerless. But', she smiled triumphantly, 'that is all changed because the law since 1981 makes all coffee-pickers equal and entitled to their own money. A mother can plan her spending and make sure she is not short. It was like we were getting in control of our own lives for the first time.'

'To Read is to Discover' cries one of the billboards of the Sandinista government. And it was true. In Marisol's house there was not a large library. But there were books that opened up a world existing outside the relentless demands of coffee-picking. There were poetry books, magical novels, and stories based on historical figures. There were the writings of Che and Fonseca that put her daily grind into a context. And there were books on health and childhood illnesses. 'I will always remember the first time I found what was wrong with my child written in a book. It was measles. I did not even know the word then. But I could recognise the fever, the sore eyes and ears, and I could see the spots. I never let that happen to my other children. I knew then to have them vaccinated. It's hard to say but at that moment I was so happy, even though my child was so sick. Because I knew other children had had exactly this, I wasn't so afraid.'

Reading is still in its infancy in Nicaragua. In 1979, 53% of the population was illiterate. One of the first campaigns undertaken by the new government was the literacy crusade of 1980. By 1983 the rate of illiteracy had dropped to 13%, winning Nicaragua the UNESCO literacy prize.[1] Illiteracy is a problem that particularly affected women, since no priority was given to female education in the days of Somoza. In 1977, 93% of women in rural zones could not read. Only 21.3% of girls attended secondary school, and only 11% went to university. In 1975, 214,597 girls and 213,993 boys received primary and secondary schooling. By 1983 these numbers had risen to 609,083 girls and 562,978 boys. Before 1979 there were no female students in agricultural, industrial or civil engineering, but in 1983 women were 18% of agricultural students and 35% of industrial and civil engineering students.[2] In addition a programme of scholarships began in 1980 to encourage women to participate in technical careers. In 1983 57% of students in technical areas were women, as were 47% of those pursuing professional qualifications.

Pre-school education has led to more freedom for women with children to pursue their own lives, and although it is not available everywhere the numbers involved are increasing. In 1983, there were 66,850 children being cared for in such centres around the country. They are run by the social welfare ministry and are usually free. Back in 1978, by contrast, only 9,000 children attended pre-school centres, and these were private and fee-paying as they are to this day in Ireland.

The literacy campaign was a good example of what could be done with sheer determination. Although only 12 million dollars was spent on it, 95,000 volunteer 'Brigadistas' were involved. First, eighty volunteers studied the teaching method and materials to be used; they then trained another 560 teachers who trained a further 7,000, and so on until all 95,000 were ready for work.[3] Owners of lorries and buses lent their vehicles to transport the volunteer teachers to remote outposts, and every community had the facility to learn provided locally, to minimise the trouble involved for busy adults. The 'Brigadistas' stayed in their assigned area for six months, sharing life with the local community.

The economic crisis caused by the Contra war, the US

trade embargo and the direction of funds away from social and infrastructural programmes has had its effect on the new literacy. Although 200,000 adults had enrolled in courses in 1984, the government now reports a fall-off in participation. This is largely due to longer working hours, as the country's production schedule has moved to an emergency 'survival' basis. It is also because many of those most enthusiastic to learn are now being drawn into the defence militias. This absorbs whatever free time is available. Nevertheless, spending on education is being maintained. Between 1979 and 1984 spending on education increased by 450%, and 1,404 new schools were built. At present, one of the projects involving thousands of foreign volunteer workers and funds from abroad is a building programme for new schools in the Sebaco valley, north of Managua.

Poverty is not something which can be made to disappear overnight, and third world levels of poverty are evident in Nicaragua. In the pre-1979 period, studies showed an 83% level of malnutrition among children; severe cases were as high as 45% in many areas.[4] Hunger and lack of basic vaccination were the big killers of children under five in that period. The women's movement began a series of 'Popular Health Days' to raise awareness about the major infectious diseases in 1980. The campaign for vaccination has been extremely successful, with 88% of children now immunised against polio and 78% against measles.[5] There has been a widening of access to health care, particularly in the rural areas, where doctors were reluctant to venture. Campaigns of popular health education, working on the lines of the literacy campaign, have mobilised 30,000 people to carry out basic tasks such as draining of stagnant water and burning rubbish. Most of these volunteers are women. In addition, two large maternity hospitals have been built in Managua since 1979, allowing poorer women access to full facilities in childbirth. Although there is huge overcrowding, hospital births have led to a significant decline in neo-natal mortality.

Dehydration and severe diarrhoea are common killers in all tropical countries. There is now a very simple solution available, a salt rehydration package, which is made available by UNICEF. Hundreds of rehydration centres have been opened up and down the country to deal with this problem, and the superstition and fear that used to surround medication is slowly waning. Of course, the Contra radio station has attacked both vaccination programmes and the rehydration solutions. They can be heard to broadcast the 'fact' that children will be transformed into godless communists by the 'injections of Tomas Borge's urine'[6]. But the practical evidence speaks loudly against such propaganda. After the first vaccination programme in 1981 (in which half a million children were inoculated) no case of polio was reported in the next two years, and measles dropped from being the fifth most common infectious disease to the thirteenth.

Drugs and medicines are often in short supply because of the trade embargo. The Nicaraguan drug industry is making a concerted attempt to supply by itself the 500 medicines in the World Health Organisation list of basic remedies for all important illnesses. Going into a chemist in Nicaragua is a very different experience from that in Ireland. Very often prescriptions cannot be filled and you must trek from one pharmacy to another in the hope of finding one which has the drug. If you have a headache, instead of an array of remedies on the shelves, you will be given four or six paracetemol wrapped in a small piece of white paper. It lacks the glamour of the advertised product, but it does the same job.

People who fall on the wrong side of the law in Nicaragua face prison sentences like anywhere else in the world. Of course, the majority of prisoners after 1979 were ex-National Guardsmen who now found themselves paying for crimes of the earlier period. A lot of these and other 'ordinary' prisoners have been given the opportunity to move to 'open' prisons, where the regime is less harsh and they can learn new skills. The rehabilitative open prison system was initiated by Tomas Borge, Minister of the Interior, who was himself subjected to torture and manacled imprisonment by Somoza. He swore then that prisoners in the new Nicaragua would be given the chance to change and start a new life.

I visited the semi-open prison of El Zapotal, about 25 kilometres from Managua. Prisoners can be transferred to such a semi-open prison, having completed one-third of their sentences. Here they have freedom to move around the grounds, and to travel around the prison farm on horseback, while working, but there is still some supervision. After a period in this prison, a person can be moved to one of the totally open prisons, where there are only one or two unarmed warders. These prisoners can come and go as they please, including travelling into the nearby town. There are now fourteen open or semi-open prisons for men in the penal system, and an open prison for women has recently been completed.

El Zapotal is a farm, where prisoners engage in pig rearing, horse breeding and tillage. The prisoners can be seen on horseback galloping the length and breadth of the land, securing fences, moving livestock, spraying crops. In addition there is a leather workshop where prisoners learn the important craft of boot and saddle making, and a photographic workshop where prisoners develop their own prints. Of the prisoners I met there many were former National Guardsmen. They told me, in an unsupervised conversation, that they were genuinely happy to be in the semi-open system and that they hoped the training would help them to get work when they were released. They seemed to be regretful about their period in the Guardia, and a few stressed that they had joined out of dire poverty, but without being committed to the Somoza regime. Outside they proudly showed me their landscaped garden crafted by their own hands, shrubs and orchids, rock plants and cacti, and cascades of purple bougainvillaea. There was no evidence of bitterness towards their gaolers, only an optimism for their individual futures.

Of course not all former Guardsmen have been so co-operative. The country's only high security prison at Tipitapa houses 2,860 inmates, of whom 2,162 are ex 'Guardia'. One thousand of these refuse to do any work, and the human rights organisation America's Watch describes their regime as 'harsh', with frequent friction over discipline, and consequent punishment such as loss of visits.

These are the most hardened prisoners, who have no regrets about their past lives, and no desire to be 'rehabilitated'. While in prison they serve their sentences in what we would view as normal prison conditions, with none of the advantages inherent in the newer system.

The Catholic Institute for International Relations, having looked in detail at the lives of prisoners in Nicaragua today, concluded: 'In a continent notorious for appalling prison conditions, where brutality and corruption are the norm, Nicaragua's penal system stands out as a genuine effort to find a more humane yet affordable alterntive. Such criticism as there is concentrates on lack of resources, which is a feature of the Nicaraguan economy as a whole and is not limited to the prison system'.

The achievement of an eight-hour working day was one of the first aims of the FSLN in government. In the cities this has been largely achieved, but in the countryside a ten-hour day and a six-day week are still commonplace. In the country, too, children still tend to carry out agricultural tasks to the detriment of their schooling. The weather is a hard taskmaster for rural Nicaraguans. The crops must be harvested before the rainy season ends, because the harsh heat of the dry season rots fruit and berries almost immediately. In the harvesting season, it is all hands on deck, because the period between being ripe and being rotten is so short. With the minimal technology available, hard work and back-bending are the necessary prerequisites of survival.

1. *Educacion en la revolucion 1979-1984*, Ministerio de Educacion, Nicaragua.
2. 'The advances achieved by the Nicaraguan women's movement', Amnlae document.
3. Diana Melrose, *Nicaragua, the Threat of a Good Example*, Oxfam.
4. 'Developments in Health Care in Nicaragua', *New England Journal of Medicine*, Vol. 307, No. 6, 5th Aug. 1982, p. 389.
5. Figures from the Nicaraguan Ministry of Health.
6. Tomas Borge is Nicaragua's Minister of the Interior, and was one of the chief policymakers of the Sandinistas in the period before 'the triumph'.

# Chains and Change

'These are the ones who will know about the new freedom for women.' Rosa points to her two youngest daughters, aged seven and ten. 'Who am I, I'm from the past. When I married, my husband was the boss. He sat at home all week, and then came to collect my salary. He always had mistresses, and once, when I had just had our fifth child, he left for six months. I took him back, because he was kind in his way. He never hit me. That was the way we thought then. I was lucky enough.'

Rosa worked all her life as a housekeeper. As such she was exempt from the labour law which restricted work to 48 hours per week, under Somoza's rule. She typically worked an eighty-four-hour week. On top of her paid work she did all the housework, because the prevailing tradition of machismo did not lend itself to sharing domestic tasks. 'Life was very hard for me. Sometimes I'd have days where I never sat down at all. I'd even eat standing up, cooking at the same time. But I'm not bitter about it. I can see already that things have changed for the better.'

Rosa was born in 1939, in a suburb on the outskirts of Managua. She left school at the age of ten and used to help her mother, who was also a housekeeper. Her first child was born in 1957, and she married the father in the following year. Altogether she had eight children, five girls and three boys. Her last daughter was born in 1980, when she was 41.

'Life was always the same when I was growing up. My mother cleaned people's houses, so I knew I would do the same. Now I don't know what my children will be. Two of my daughters have gone on to secondary school, and they might work in offices. I know they will expect to be treated as equals by whomever they marry', says Rosa. Education is certainly one of the key instruments for the changes in women's lives. In 1977, only twenty-one per cent of girls received secondary education, and only eleven per cent attended university. There were no official literacy programmes, and in rural areas ninety-three per cent of women were illiterate. This gave men a huge power in society; they were legally responsible for their wives and could decide on everything, including where the family would live and where the children would work or be educated. It was relatively easy for men to divorce their wives, but not the other way round. If a woman was unfaithful even once, she could be accused of 'adultery' and divorced. Such minor indiscretions by husbands had no legal recourse, and a woman was entitled to divorce only if her husband maintained a mistress in the conjugal residence, 'publicly and scandalously' (Article 130 of the Penal Code).

class background. She is not an unhappy person, but she has had a tremendously hard life. A lot of her aspirations were through her children, and the fun she got out of them was the main pleasure in her life. She expressed amazement at the number of Western women (myself included) who would reach thirty without having any children. 'They are the best thing for me. I never thought about whether I would have children or how. They just started to come and they had to be minded. I would not like to have left it too late to have any ...' Her smile accompanying this hint was familiar in conversations with Nicaraguan women. It was perhaps the biggest cultural difference between us. I would regard Rosa's 23 years of childbearing as hardship. She genuinely feared I was going to miss life's greatest experience for a woman.

Women of Rosa's age are in the transition between two societies. They have the memories of a life of repression, as recently as the 1970s. They can see the difficulties for the new society in the making, especially the shortages and the conscription for the war. 'I hate to see young boys having to fight; but I'm hoping that the war will end, and the queues will stop, and our young people will get some advantages from the change of government', Rosa finished by saying.

One writer has summarised the position for women in Nicaragua in the Somoza period as follows; 'To be a poor woman in Nicaragua in the 1970s, after thirty or more years of dependent "development", meant to expect to live to be about fifty. To be poor and female meant a three-out-of-ten chance of never attending school, and becoming one of every two over the age of ten who remained functionally illiterate. To be poor also meant to end childhood and adolescence abruptly at or shortly after puberty with a first pregnancy, usually out of wedlock. To be a woman, aged 34, meant having reached advanced middle age. In the rural areas, such a woman could expect to have been pregnant an average of eight times, although only three or four of her children would still be alive. In the more urbanised Department of Managua about half of the single mothers of comparable age could count on having three of five children alive. The vast majority would be matriarchs, probably not by choice, with responsibility for maintaining the household.'[1]

These statistics tell some of the story. The atmosphere of daily life was no better. Inside the home, there was domestic violence and alcoholism. In the streets, there was repression, and fear of rape. Many women were forced into prostitution by poverty, and the image of women portrayed in advertising was degraded and degrading. Married women, or women cohabiting with men, rarely received help in housework, and men spent time quite openly with women other than their downtrodden wives. Although women had the right to vote, there were no women in the National Assembly.

Myself and another Irish woman, Eadaoin, walked down the potholed road of Riguero, one day. The houses were makeshift and every door was wide open. The sanctity of privacy is easily sacrificed to the additional air and space afforded by an open door. We sat up at a local bar to sample the local 'fresco' (fruit juice). There were two women behind the counter, a mother and daughter. The daughter had three children, two aged about seven and five and a chubby little baby who, we were told, was seven months old. While the other children were distinctly the colour of their mother, this baby was pale. 'La chelita' (the little pale one) smiled her grandmother indulgently. She told us that the baby's father was an American. I remember being really amazed by the lack of bitterness shown to this man. 'He had to return home', the young woman said with a smile. But both women were obviously happy and charmed at this little addition to their female household. Perhaps the lack of anger comes from a powerlessness to make men responsible for their children. Everywhere I went, here or in El Salvador, I saw hundreds of blue-eyed blondes integrated into the community without any sense of strangeness.

But perhaps the lack of anger comes from something else. There is a popular Nicaraguan saying: 'mejor sola que mal acompañada', 'Better alone than badly accompanied'. A third of Nicaragua's families are headed by women, and I think that women are happier rearing their children alone rather than being burdened by a drunken or recalcitrant husband. Grandmothers seem to play a major role in these women's lives, and it was very common to come across extended families where the older family members reared the young children, leaving the mother free to earn the necessary income.

As early as 1967, the FSLN was addressing the problem of women's underprivileged role in society. Their platform for that year pinpointed the main problem areas as: 'unequal wages, double workload (inside and outside of the home), isolation from political and social participation, use as a sexual object and legal discrimination'[2]. The lead in fighting for women's rights came from within the movement for overall social change, rather than in the United States and Western Europe where women autonomously began to organise themselves, on feminist issues. In 1977 the Association of Women Confronting the National Problem (Ampronac) was established, around demands such as equal pay, equal rights and an end to sex objectification. They also organised against the rule of Somoza, and highlighted human rights violations. And they provided a logistical base for the FSLN, acting as messengers, hiding Sandinistas on the run and using warning codes (such as banging on pots and pans) to indicate the arrival of the Guardia. By 1979 many women had become FSLN activists, and it is estimated that between one quarter and a third of combatants were women. On the day the Sandinistas marched victoriously into Managua, 19 July, 1979, Ampronac changed its name and its organisation to AMNLAE (the Luisa Amanda Espinoza Nicaraguan women's association). The movement was now dedicated to the first woman who had died in the struggle against Somoza.

Since 1979, Amnlae, which is separate from the FSLN but sees itself as fighting the same battle, has organised throughout the country. In April 1980, it had 17,000 members and by October 1981 this had risen to 25,000. The mainstays of its organisation are the work committees, which organise women in groups of three to ten, to express their views in non-threatening situations. The demand for these groups was shown in the early years, when the number of them grew from 490 to 1981 to 817 in 1982. A particular priority is to organise rural women. The Amnlae members I spoke to all pointed out that here was where the oppression was deepest and where women were most isolated from each other. At the First Conference of Women Rural Workers Jaime Wheelock, the Commandante in charge of Agrarian Reform, put it this way; 'How many times we arrived in a peasant home where the woman didn't speak with us because she would not leave the kitchen'. The role and view that Amnlae sees for itself is best summed up in the words of Lea Guido, former Nicaraguan Health Minister and President of the Pan American Health Organisation: 'Active militancy has shown us the true dimension of our oppression: its economic roots, its social limitations and its ideological justification. This has helped us to understand that women's liberation is a joint task. Our role is to lay the foundation by becoming conscious of our condition. We must name the problem, recognise it in all its forms and work to change it'.

One of those who came to the Sandinista Front through the recognition of woman's oppression is Sofia

Montenegro. She is now a journalist with *Barricada*, the FSLN's daily newspaper, and is 32 years of age. Her story is a pretty remarkable one. Her father was a major in Somoza's regime, and her eldest brother a lieutenant colonel in his army. She went to university to study journalism, and began to read about feminism. She had become aware that women were powerless in Nicaragua, but now she could see in black and white how universal that experience was. 'As a woman I rebelled', she told me, 'then I found through reading that it was not me who was crazy. My surprise was to find out that women all over the world felt the same rage. I began to read Marx and Engels too, and then I became convinced of the need to change the regime, that would be the only way to change life for women.'

She soon became actively involved with the FSLN. 'I thought of getting involved in the armed struggle, but because of who I was, I was most useful to get information. My brother would talk in the house, about troop movements and the like, and I would pass on the information. I also ran a security house for guerillas on the run, and I was chauffeur, and smuggled arms. If the Guardia stopped me I would say, "How dare you try to search me, do you not know who my father and brother are?" I used to worry about it, but I knew how vicious the regime was, and I wanted to help change it. Many families were divided like this, and it was a generation gap too.'

Her father, who had fought against Sandino with the Americans back in the 1930s, died a year before the Sandinista triumph. The family really split in 1979. Her brother was arrested, and was due to face trial for crimes committed as a member of the Guardia, but he was shot trying to escape custody just three months later. 'My mother had asked me to help my brother escape but I had to say no, because I could not help any of Somoza's Guardia to escape. It took a long time for my mother to forgive me for that. For her he was her son, her first son, and she wouldn't believe the stories about him. It would have been worse for her if he had faced trial, and she would have seen hundreds of witnesses giving evidence of his brutality against them. He would have got thirty years in prison, the highest sentence that can be given here. It was very hard for me to refuse to help him, but I really do believe that he would have formed the embryo of a new fascist leadership, to get the dictatorship back. He had the leadership, training and brains. He knew the laws of war and that he had lost. He told me he didn't want to see me or my mother, to leave him to himself. I think he provoked being shot, because he was too proud to face trial.'

Sofia Montenegro struck me as a highly committed Sandinista, and a tireless worker for the cause of women less privileged than herself. I found it hard to come to terms with the harsh decisions she had made, and even with her informant role in the pre-revolutionary period. There is no doubt that she had been marked by what she had come through, and there was a residual sadness about her. But as an activist, she was involved in the shaping of the new Nicaragua, and had no doubt that her contribution could help to shape a better world for those around her. She had been one of those who insisted that women's equality be enshrined as a principle of the Constitution, ranking with anti-imperialism. She was involved in organising sex education in the schools, 'even though the church screamed about it', and her articles on illegal abortion led to the decriminalisation of abortion under the new Constitution. She pointed out that at least one hundred women were having abortions every month, regardless of the law, and that their health and even their lives were in danger. She spoke to women who were admitted to casualty wards in hospitals after unsuccessful abortions, and quoted one gynaecologist as saying, 'It is not a matter of class or ideology here, it is a matter of saving the lives of women who don't want to have the baby they are expecting'. Her writing and her work are greatly respected in Nicaragua, and she exudes the confidence of someone who can get things done.

She is adamant that women need to maintain their own organisation to look after their own demands. 'Women have specific needs, which are really human needs, but no matter how revolutionary the people running the government and the unions are, you must remember that they are men. Only women have the political will to organise and change things for themselves. But having said that, we now know what it's like to be free, to fly, to dream, this is what human beings cannot live without. For years, up to 1979, we had martial law and curfew at 8 o'clock. People locked themselves in their houses and spoke quietly. Now you can wander home drunk at 4 o'clock in the morning. A policeman will pick you up, say "why are you drunk?", bring you to jail and give you soup. In former times you would be dead. That's the difference. Now we can go into a cabildo [cabildo abierto, open meeting] and say to Daniel Ortega, I don't like that paragraph in the Constitution. It's taken us 50,000 deaths to get our freedom over 500 years. We mean to keep it.'

The family have been somewhat reconciled over the years, though each going their separate ways. Sofia has two sisters in Miami, who think she is mad to stay in Nicaragua because of the material hardship. She has one brother in Mexico, one in Panama married to a Panamanian, one studying in Leningrad, and one in Nicaragua with her. It took her five years to earn her mother's forgiveness for not helping her brother to escape, but now she too has started, at 71, to get involved in community work in her own locality. And she knows that even in today's Nicaragua, she needs her daughter to take care of her in her old age.

More than 30 per cent of Nicaraguan women are rearing children on their own. In Managua the rate is over 50%. Sometimes this is because women choose to have and rear children alone, or because fathers have gone away to work or to fight. In a great number of cases, the men just leave after a couple of years, and go off with another woman. But in most cases the problem is that men have traditionally refused to acknowledge paternity, and therefore not supported their children. Amnlae has targetted this as the major obstacle to women's freedom, pointing out that women who are bogged down trying to survive with their children are not free to make any real choices about their lives. Before the fall of Somoza in 1979, it was illegal to have paternity investigated. The first law brought in by the Sandinista government established a tribunal on paternity. In the future, the rearing of children was to be the joint responsibility of both parents, which meant on the one hand, that where the father was present he would no longer have the total decision on where to live, the children's education, etc. and that where he was not present, he would be obliged to support his children financially.

Miriam was a case in point. Now aged twenty-one, she found herself three years ago with two children, alone, illiterate and working a strenuous ten-hour day picking coffee to support them. The father of her children was a well-to-do private farmer with a legal family, and a number of illegitimate children in the area. She took him to the new tribunal, got maintenance and with her new found freedom cut her working hours and went to school. She is now a capable and articulate representative of farm workers. 'Learning to read was the best thing that ever happened to me,' she told me. 'Now I don't have to worry about missing something important at a meeting, I can check back on minutes, I can read the newspapers. And I know I won't let anyone down when I speak.'

She spends her days travelling around the state coffee farms and peasant co-ops, listening to people's grievances and negotiating for them with government and the coffee distributors. It's interesting work, but her days are long. Her youngest child is in the state nursery and the older boy in the town's national school. I'm amazed by the number of women working outside the home, despite the average family size of six or seven children. 'It was like that even before the revolution', says Miriam, 'Women always had to work, because the money was needed. The difference was that then women would close the door of their hut, leaving the children there, and spend all day worrying if they were all right. Now each farm has a nursery, so the children are happy and not sick so often.' Maternity leave exists now for mothers in the city and country — forty-five days before the birth and ninety days after.

The area of maternity care demonstrates some of the gaps between the huge aspirations of the new Nicaragua and the daily grind of shortages of building materials and medical supplies. In the main maternity hospital in Managua, there are often two women to a bed, one at the top and one at the foot, each trying to feed her new-born baby and recover before going home. There has been a big increase in the number of hospital births in the last ten years, with a corresponding decline in infant mortality. Some new hospitals have been built, but the demand far exceeds the supply of hospital beds, a situation worsened by the needs of the war wounded.

Alongside this hardship exists an experiment unprecedented in conditions of underdevelopment, yet representing the hope of change so vital to Nicaraguan's morale. In Esteli, at the edge of the Northern war zone, there is a centre for natural childbirth which prepares women with exercises, nutrients and herbs for the experience ahead. It places its emphasis on knowledge, confidence and demystifying labour. It is run by a Chilean exile, Suzannah Veraguas, and the centre buzzes with her enthusiasm. 'Here we encourage women to argue with their doctors, to demand answers to their questions and to feel less afraid of what lies ahead of them.' On the walls are sculpted replicas and photographs of the various stages of pregnancy. These were contributed by a group of American feminists called 'Madre' who help to support the centre. It is ironic that their small voluntary contribution provides a beacon in a darkness spread by the American government's policy of war and attrition. There are a number of bedrooms in the centre, and Suzannah says that these are used by women in the last days of pregnancy to get a well-earned rest in surroundings of comfort and hygiene. They are also used by women whose husbands are unsupportive or downright hostile. On the wall outside the centre is a large and cheery mural of a mother and child. 'Natural childbirth is the best start for the new being', says Tomas Borge, the Sandinista leader who was himself brutally tortured by Somoza's National Guard, and whose wife was raped by them. He is the ideological source for much of the newest and most experimental thinking in the Nicaraguan process.

Talking to some of the mothers who came in for classes, I was struck by the contrasting fear and confidence within them. They knew very little about the process of childbirth itself, and one woman told me that she had been told that if you spoke about menstruation, it would stop i.e. you would become pregnant. This project, by contrast, was well rooted in the late twentieth century. The women were encouraged to demand an accompanying person at the delivery, something which many doctors are unhappy about. (As many as 80 per cent want their mothers present, but 10-15 per cent of husbands or companeros now attend. Susannah says most of them are young and have learnt attitudes of involvement and responsibility while doing their military service.) Women who are having hospital births are encouraged to 'push' at their own pace, and are made aware of the different drugs used. They can then insist on a drug-free labour if they so desire.

On the basic economic level, women's lives have improved considerably in the last decade, despite the continuing shortages. Women and men are given equal rights in law, property and work in the new Constitution. Women have a 50 per cent say in the disposal of the family home in a separation, they are entitled to widow's and orphans' support even where formal marriage did not exist. Single women may now adopt children — formerly only couples who were married for ten years, and infertile, could do so.

In 1977 women represented 26% of the economically-active population in the cities, and 15% in the countryside.[3] By 1983 the comparable figures were 41.6% in the cities and 48.6% in the country.[4] The early legislation banning the use of women to sell products and prohibiting prostitution have had various degrees of success. The advertising legislation passed the day after the Sandinista triumph is implemented strictly and adhered to. While prostitution has declined, many women still fall back on it to earn a livelihood, especially recently, as the economic crisis has become so severe. Amnlae has organised a number of collectives for former prostitutes to teach them skills such as dressmaking, cooking and arts and crafts.[5] For working women there are 137 childcare centres operating in the cities and fifty on the state farms. Each large farm has a nursery attached, with trained personnel employed. The freeing of women to work outside the home is reflected in the fact that 25% of those unionised are now women.

Some of the best conversations I had with Nicaraguan women took place at the big outdoor sinks where women came together to wash clothes and chat. Sheer muscle power on the corrugated stone was used with ordinary soap to produce gleaming clothes worthy of a Persil advertisement. They were amazed that I had reached the ripe old age of thirty-one without being able to wash my jeans properly. But the gossip was always good, between the jibes.

One day the subject of family planning came up. While the women were all in favour of pills and condoms being available, they pointed out that it was not as straight-forward an issue as it would be in Ireland. 'Look at El Salvador', one said to me. 'Their poor women are told they will only get economic help if they agree to be sterilised. That's not right.' 'And the contraception injection [Depo Provera] can make women very sick', commented another. I asked about the Catholic Church's objections, and yes, they agreed that that would influence some of them. But they did feel that even if they would not use the pill themselves, it was right that it should be available to anyone wanting it. Miriam chipped in at this point to say that the clause in the Constitution dealing with family planning stated that Nicaraguans should have the freedom 'to decide responsibly and freely how many children they want to have and the moment in their life they want to have them'. 'Of course', she continued, 'very often a husband thinks he is choosing to have children, while his wife is choosing not to.' The laughter this evoked made me think that a lot of Nicaraguan women were avoiding taking their husbands on in regard to the number of children they should have. Nicaraguan men tend to want big families to prove themselves in machismo. Many women are obviously deciding when they have enough children and getting on with using contraception themselves.

Nicaraguan women become sexually active very young, 38.28% between the ages of fourteen and sixteen and 72.72% by the age of nineteen.[6] This is customary in poor Latin American countries, but it may also be due in part to over-crowding. It is estimated that in the poorer parts of

Managua 65% of houses have only one bedroom. Six or seven people would sleep in this room. This lack of space means that young people learn about sex early. The commonest forms of contraception used are the contraceptive pill and the IUD. Condoms are not popular, probably because of the difficulty of involving men in family planning at this stage. Sterilisation is permitted under certain circumstances, among them that both partners agree, that the woman is at a certain age, and that she already had some children. This is to prevent world planned parenthood organisations convincing young women to be sterilised in exchanged for inducements.

Although family planning is widely available, and sex education has been taught in the schools since 1983, Nicaraguans still tend to like having a lot of children. In Managua, where one third of the population lives, the average family has five children; in other cities the average is 5 to 6, while on the Atlantic Coast the median number is 6 to 7.[7] The Child Support Law (July 1982) ensures that women receive some economic assistance from the father in the rearing of children. It states that both parents 'must contribute within their means to the support of the family. This can be in the form of money, goods or household tasks. And with regard to the last category all family members, regardless of sex, who are capable of doing so, must contribute to household tasks'. At meal times, Nicaraguan radio announcers can be heard to urge husbands to help with housework, cooking and washing up.

While efforts like this show the reality of the commitment to women's equality, the economic backwardness of the country makes the progress patchy and uneven, with some advances which are way beyond Western women, and in other places a grinding and seemingly immutable oppression. The area of domestic violence is a case in point. It is still the most common reason for divorce and separation in Nicaragua. The commonest reasons for battering, according to Rosa Maria Zelaya of the Office of Family Protection, are jealousy, disapproval of political or community involvement and alcoholism. While the first and last causes are very typical of a society hidebound by machismo, the second category is interesting. It shows a reaction by some men to the new-found confidence and social involvement of women. The more common such involvement becomes, the more they will be forced to accept it. Ramon, a personnel manager in a Managuan factory, put it this way; 'My wife has changed a lot in these years. I see her as much more confident. Before she never had men friends, only women. Now she does. I have to admit that it has been difficult for me to accept this. I am jealous. But sometimes I am delighted that my wife is a woman and not a little girl dependent on me. In the neighbourhood, she has many responsibilities that even I am not fully aware of.' Mariana, a secretary in a communications office, commented: 'I was just a housewife for twenty years. After the victory, listening to other women talk about their participation in various tasks, I began to feel useless. I could only talk about the price of rice and vegetables. I was just the wife of so-and-so. My husband encouraged me to get involved in the Literacy crusade. That was my school and the school for many women like me. It made me realise my capabilities and helped me to overcome a mountain of complexes and inhibitions.'[8]

The most notable transformation has indeed been in the areas of literacy and health. More than one million people, or 40 per cent of the population, are participating in one or other of the educational programmes available. 53% of these students are women. Health campaigns have concentrated on education on nutrition, developing preventive medicine and basic hygiene, and carrying out immunisations against preventable disease. The programme of maternal infant care is very significant. The number of medical consultations in this area increased by 263.3% between 1977 and 1983.[9]

The women's movement has established a number of legal offices throughout the country to help women to assert and establish their new legal entitlements. Maria Esperanza Nieta is a former judge, and now runs the women's legal office in Managua. 'Sadly mistreatment (i.e wife battering) is the major problem reported to us. Nicaraguan men have to change and be made aware that they can no longer get away with mistreating their wives, that society will not accept it,' she said. 'We will take the case for a woman right through the judicial system, providing her with medical assistance, making the complaint to the police and going to court with her'. Domestic violence is a criminal offence to which a sentence of six months to five years attaches. 'Sometimes women are slow to press charges, but just want to give their violent husbands a fright. If this is the case we can insist on him seeing a psychologist or psychiatrist. Surprisingly, the shame of this often prevents a recurrence of the violence.' The whole society is seen to have a role in preventing the mistreatment of children. A neighbour who observes abuse of children can report it and it is then legally investigated. While all of this may seem to indicate a very weak social position for women in Nicaraguan society, it is indicative of the uneven nature of the gains being made. Nicaragua is still an underdeveloped country, with many of the hallmarks which accompany such poverty. And before we rest on laurels of superiority we should remember that only twenty years ago, before the AIM group brought the problem into the open, wife battering was not discussed or recognised in Ireland.

The war against the US-backed Contra forces has eaten up massive material and human resources in Nicaragua. The ambitious social programmes in the area of health and education have remained on the back burner since 1983, when the war intensified. The economy is on a survival footing, and every young man must do military service for two years. Some sections of the women's movement were demanding conscription for women to allow them a fully equal place in the defence of their country, but women's involvement in the army remains on a voluntary basis. Those women who do join up are integrated totally, and fight on equal terms with their male colleagues. Unlike the Irish army, they are not relegated to the areas of cooking and first aid. A large and growing number of women are joining the army, and the part-time popular militias. In order to understand this, we need to remember that the whole popular culture is based around the historic defiance of American military might, the notion of an army that is a part of the people, and the place of the Sandinista martyrs in people's memories.

Perhaps I can best explain the feeling of this by telling about two women I met while travelling in the Northern part of Nicaragua. The Casa de la Cultura in Esteli is housed in a mansion that was owned by one of Somoza's friends. Through the downstairs living-room is a large patio with swimming pool, what was a private bar and a magnificent moss garden which breathes cool damp air. One can imagine the degenerate parties that took place in the heyday of the dictatorship, the high stools at the gaudy cocktail bar, the poolside couches, and the vast interior of the house itself. Now the pool is full of local children, the bar empty and disused. The house teems with artefacts, posters and paintings, and upstairs children swing their hips as they learn the basic steps of mariachi dancing.

The Museum of Heroes and Martyrs of the Revolution stands in a room at the end of the upstairs hallway. Unlike our notion of what constitutes a museum, the emphasis here is on photographs of those killed — line upon line of young and not so young faces, of the handsome and suave, of the poor and illiterate, of youthful beauty and stocky maternalism. 'We shall never forget our martyrs' states one of the most popular Sandinista slogans. Esteli rose against the Somoza regime twice before the final triumph, in September 1978 and April 1979. Then in July 1979 more fighters and civilians were killed in the final offensive. And there were those who died within days of the victory of July 19th, of wounds inflicted in the preceding period.

Looking at the rows of faces, I was wondering about the separate dreams of each one, ambition, love, the desire to carry through the change. Maria Lorenza Gomez touched me on the elbow and pointed me in the direction of a picture further down the wall. It was her son, Nelson Ruiz Gomez, killed in April 1979. He was twenty, with that pale beauty of inspired youth. She told me quietly about his beliefs, his involvement with the FSLN, about his reading political books instead of doing his schoolwork, of his love of Nicaragua and his kindness to her. With tears in her eyes she remembered how the Guardia surrounded the town and bombarded it with shells from the nearby hills. They were afraid to come into the town and face the people in combat. Her son was hit by an army shell, and she never saw him alive again. She works in the museum most days, saying that she finds it less upsetting to think about him and talk about him than to be cut off. Perhaps the deaths of all those young people would be a guarantee against a tyrant ever gaining control again. Despite what she had been through Maria Gomez looked young and sturdy, with that unlined complexion so typical of Nicaraguan women of middle age. She had two other children, a son and a daughter. Her son worked in the local hospital, her daughter was now a mother herself and served in a local shop. She shook her head solemnly at me: 'Such a small family I had'.

That same day, I found the bookshop run by the mother of the famous martyr poet, Leonel Rugama. It was in a little street just off the main square. A sign hanging outside said simply, 'Rugama bookshop' and inside there was an oil painting of the young man. Candida de Rugama was a tiny woman. She had been a schoolmistress, her husband a carpenter. She had that precise loveliness that comes of an open intelligence. She was delighted to meet someone from Ireland. She had heard of the political situation there, and asked me about the North. She had had a visit that morning from a Japanese woman and she recorded all her visitors and their country in a book which she glanced over happily.

Leonel Rugama was one of Nicaragua's most promising poets. He was also an accomplished mathematician, and a member of the Frente Sandinista. In 1970 he was tracked by the forces of the National Guard to a house in Managua where he was staying with some other guerillas. It was decided to make an example of him. The television cameras were brought along, the house was surrounded by tanks and marksmen, but the propaganda stunt went badly wrong for Somoza. The handful of guerillas fought back and refused to give up. The battle went on for several hours, and instead of quelling dissent it inspired people as they watched at home, showing that a fight back was possible against the military might of the state. Eventually, only Leonel Rugama remained alive inside the house. He was called on to surrender. 'Que se rinde tu madre', he shouted back, which is a colloquial and not very polite way of saying 'never'. This expression has been adopted into the FSLN folklore, as an expression of resistance to US aggression. The building was stormed and the poet was killed. He was just twenty-one.

The political tradition of martyrdom is something we in Ireland can understand. The shooting of the 1916 leaders gave them a national profile and sympathy that the British Government had not expected. In Nicaragua, women are involved in this political work, reminding the new generations of the suffering that went into creating a state free of fear, and based on human values. It is by no means the only involvement of women in the Nicaraguan process, but it is one that they themselves would see as key to the survival of this stage of their struggle.

A number of women have achieved positions of national importance within Nicaragua. Dora Maria Tellez was a Sandinista fighter before 1979. She was second in command to Eden Pastora in the famous 1978 assault on the National Palace, which led to the exchange of members of Somoza's assembly for political prisoners, including Tomas Borge. She became Minister for Health in the new government. Doris Tijerino is the head of Police and Security, a very unusual post for a woman to hold in the macho culture of Latin America. Nora Astorga was rated as Nicaragua's most capable foreign diplomat before her untimely death in 1988. The government tried to install her as Ambassador to the United States, but it was a measure of her ability that she was unacceptable to the US administration in that role. She then became Nicaragua's delegate to the United Nations, which allowed her to wield influence in Washington. Claudia Chamorro is Nicaragua's ambassador to Costa Rica, a post of fundamental importance in the present attempts to galvanise a united regional approach in opposition to US domination. Her famous family included the liberal martyr Pedro Chamorro, whose death at the hands of Somoza's National Guard many regard as a turning point in the struggle. In this generation the family is divided, with one brother in the leadership of the Contras and another brother (who edits *Barricada*) in support of the Nicaraguan government.

These women are the exception. The leaders of the Frente Sandinista are well aware of this and hope that the new generation will see more women in positions of leadership. They point out that in the pre-revolutionary period women suffered most from illiteracy. Their opinions were worth nothing before the law. Bad health and poor nutrition made survival itself a struggle. It is little wonder that those women who came to prominence did so as exceptions rather than the norm. Attitudes do change slowly, and though the women's organisations now give confidence and support to individual women, it will take some time for women to be fully integrated in the national leadership of their country. But the will to so include them is there now, at least.[10]

1. Susan E. Ramirez Horton, *The Role of Women in the Nicaraguan Revolution*.
2. *Envio*, 2nd July 1983.
3. Nicaraguan Central Bank Report, 1978.
4. Nicaraguan Household Survey, 1983.
5. 'Women in Nicaragua: A Revolution within a Revolution', *Envio*, July 1983.
6. 'Women in Nicaragua', *Envio*.
7. 'Matriarchy-Patriarchy', a study carried out by J. G. Moncada in 1977.
8. Quoted in 'The Nicaraguan Family in a Time of Transition', *Envio*, April 1984.
9. 'The Nicaraguan Family in a Time of Transition', *Envio*.
10. At present 22% of the members of the FSLN are women, as are 37% of those holding regional and departmental administrative positions. Women hold 24.6% of middle-level executive posts, yet there is still not one woman among the nine commanders of the FSLN directorate.

# Hungering for God and Bread

It was a hot Good Friday in Rivas in southern Nicaragua. The large dusty church presided over the green square in front of it, and a huge crowd had gathered, singing. The women were dressed in purple dresses or blouses. The children had the marks of the crown of thorns painted on their heads, with rather gory spatterings of blood dripping from them. The whole town was out. It was about one o'clock in the day.

For the next three hours this huge procession wended its way around the town and surrounding countryside, to arrive back to the church for the long ceremony of the day. The devotion was total. At the front of the march six men carried a huge statue of Christ, carrying his cross. His hair was lifelike, his clothing of torn red and brown velvet. The singing was led by a brass band, composed mainly of Sandinista policemen in their uniforms. Tubas, trumpets and cymbals rang out the convictions of the people of Rivas, that the suffering Christ would soon be triumphant.

I was too faint-hearted to join the Rivas procession in the baking heat, because I had been warned of its length. As the sounds of hymn-singing receded into the distance, I found myself quite alone in an empty town. I went into the church. On the dome in front of the high altar, I found a painting which made my already busy head reel. It depicted a stormy sea, in which the grey battleships of Communismo, Anarchismo and Materialismo foundered on the rocks of the Faith of the People. The letters were eight to ten foot high, and every detail was clear from the seats in the church. It struck me that this rather graphic piece of anti-communism must have dated from the 1930s. It represented one side in the debate within the church on social equality and the Catholic message. That view sits side by side with the church activists of the Basic Christian communities who are implementing Vatican Two's Option for the Poor, by living among Nicaragua's poorest citizens. They believe that the church must vocally support improvements in the lives of the poor, in the here and now. They say the poor live closest to Christ's real message in the modern world. The divided church suddenly seemed very real.

One of the earliest pronouncements of the new FSLN government was on religion. It stated that the freedom to profess a religious faith was an inalienable human right, which would be guaranteed. This was important to put people's minds at ease, since many of the leaders of the Sandinistas were avowed atheists and agnostics. They wanted people to know that they had no intention of trying to undermine anyone's convictions. And so it has remained. Christians and non-believers in the Sandinista Front have worked together for their common social goals.

The centrality of religion was, in fact, reflected in the appointment of four priests to posts within the new government. And the Catholic Church's pastoral letter of 1979 ('A Christian Commitment for a new Nicaragua') welcomed the climate of change. On the subject of the socialist nature of the new government the pastoral declared: 'If the interests of the majority of Nicaraguans are paramount and if it includes an economic system with national interests in mind, we have no objection'.

This is not to say that relations between the state and the church have been completely equable. Certain sections of the church have been involved in denouncing the political and economic process that is Sandinismo. The FSLN policy on religion deems it to be a personal matter, the responsibility of individuals, churches and the associations that are organised for religious purposes. Although there are many informal overlaps between the work of the churches and the work of the state, the church receives no sponsorship or backing from the government. Nevertheless Christian schools, of which there are 152 Catholic and 21 Protestant, do receive assistance from the Ministry of Education.

There has been no fall-off of interest in religion in the years following the 'triumph'. The following table demonstrates a numerical growth, in fact, in congregations, vocations, and places of training for the priesthood and religious life.

## RELIGION

| | 1979 | 1986 | % increase |
|---|---|---|---|
| Churches | 167 | 178 | 6.7 |
| Congregations | 54 | 82 | 50 |
| Priests | 293 | 430 | 44 |
| Monks/Nuns | 549 | 856 | 55 |
| Seminaries | 2 | 8 | 400 |
| Protestant Church | 46 (incl. | 85 (incl. | 84 (churches) |
| Denominations | 1,500 | 2,000 | 33 (clergy) |
| | clergymen) | clergymen) | |

* The evangelical churches account for nearly 15% of the country's Christians. The Assemblies of God is the largest evangelical denomination, with 6,000 followers and 400 places of worship (not included in the churches in the above table).

The total number of places of worship is about 1,500.

*Source:* Speech by Daniel Ortega at 25th Anniversary ceremony 8.11.86, *Envio,* December 1986 p. 15.

There has been a huge increase in the activity of evangelical churches since 1979. Then 95% of the population were Catholic, now the percentage is 85%. Evangelical singing can be heard all over Managua in the evening time. Their message is one of passivity and fatalism, which appears attractive in the situation of crisis prevailing. While most Nicaraguans are Catholic, there are great differences among them. As in Ireland, Nicaraguan

Catholics often digress from the moral strictures imposed by the international church. Sexual expression is not confined to marriage, and contraception is freely available and widely used.

The major differences are not in this area at all, but in the area of politics, where there has been divergence between the hierarchy appointed by Rome and the Christian base communities, often labelled the 'popular church'. Pope John Paul II has involved himself publicly in these debates and has been seen to admonish priests and nuns who see their role as defending the rights of the poor. In his letter of 29 June, 1982 to the Nicaraguan bishops he stated: 'The Church in Nicaragua has the great responsibility of being a sacrament, that is to say, the sign and instrument of unity in the country ... united in the shared Gospel ideals of justice, peace, solidarity, communion and participation, without being irrevocably divided by contingent choices arising from systems, movements, parties or organisations'. He went on to say that it was 'absurd and dangerous to imagine a "popular" or "People's" church alongside, not to say in opposition to the church built up round the bishop'. This very polemical tone to an issue of great sensitivity within Nicaragua was the start of a concerted campaign by a part of the hierarchy in Nicaragua against the Nicaraguan government, and by extension, against members of the church who had been working closely with the government in their various social programmes.

The two major figures to enlist the Pope's support in this way were Bishop Obando Y Bravo, Bishop of Managua and now Cardinal, and Bishop Vega, who regularly preached to the Contra troops and backers in Miami. They represent a conservative force in the Church, one which is opposed to changes leading to greater social equity. They view such moves as communistic in their intent and result, and have worked hard to galvanise Nicaraguan Catholics into an anti-government force. They might not have expected the Vatican to intervene on their side in such a direct way, but John Paul II is a crusading conservative himself and was happy to use his position to send advice from Rome. During his visit to Nicaragua in 1983, he openly chided the priests participating in the Nicaraguan government. This is part of an overall strategy of attacking the supporters of 'liberation theology' within the church, a theology conceived and widely followed in the Latin American congregations.

The famous pastoral letter of 1982 went on to decry the notion of a people's church: 'Since the term "people" easily takes on a markedly social and political content, it means a church incarnated in the people's organisations, a church marked by ideologies placed at the service of the people's claims and programmes and struggles, and naturally at war with groups considered not to belong to the people ... the concept of a "people's church" can only with difficulty avoid taking on strongly ideological overtones, deriving from a particular radical politics, of class struggle and of an acceptance of the use of violence in order to accomplish certain ends'. The Pope concluded that such a church was 'a grave deviation from Jesus Christ's will and his plan of salvation.'

The Pope saw the Nicaraguan people as, in his own words, hungering for God (a message repeated in Catholic billboard advertising all over Managua). The reply of the Basic Christian communities was to say, 'We hunger for God, but we also hunger for bread'. They went on: 'Our country is only just beginning to lift itself out of centuries of stagnation. It is beginning to make the slow journey towards its cultural, economic and political liberation. And yet we cannot rebuild it in peace. Others do not want us to be ourselves, to be free, but we are determined that we shall be'. They talked about the Christians of today meeting like the early disciples in the catacombs and in dug-outs, but today what the Christian had to fear was the military and the death squads of repressive Latin American regimes. Their involvement in the new Nicaraguan process, by contrast, gave them an optimism: 'Because we are poor we have hope. We have learnt that Jesus was a poor man and that the poor were his favourites; it was to them that he entrusted the gospel'.

In the early 1980s, the US State Department was placing a lot of pressure on American bishops to speak out against the 'terrible repression of religion in Nicaragua'. This contention does not have much currency today. International opinion is aware that the churches are flourishing in the new Nicaragua, that priests and bishops travel freely (including Cardinal Obando Y Bravo, despite his stated opposition to the government), and public religous processions are commonplace. Nevertheless, the debate in the church does reflect the debate in Nicaraguan society generally, about the role of the Sandinista government, social change, moral issues and the war with the Contras. The Catholic Church hierarchy, whether or not it actually receives funding from the CIA (a matter which is hotly disputed), does find itself echoing the points raised in a dossier compiled by the US State Department and quoted by the Contra leadership. Most nuns, priests, and church lay people, on the other hand, tend to support the new process.

Two American missionaries that I met in Nicaragua seemed to underline this distinction between the 'two churches'. Rama was the last town before the river journey across to Bluefields. In the centre of Nicaragua, it was surrounded on all sides by jungle where the Contras had most of their bases. It was a quiet, isolated town, like a frontier town in an Amrican Western. As I walked into the local hotel, I could hear the swing doors slamming back and forth behind me, while all eyes turned to slowly consider me. Walking through the town it was the same. Footsteps. Then silence. A greeting. More silence.

In a doorway, a local priest stood watching the children carry their shopping home. He said 'Hello' and called me over. He was North American and seemed to be in his late fifties. He had been in Nicaragua since the 1960s, and had lived through the Somoza period. He felt that things had been bad enough in those years, but not as bad as many people made out. His main work was with the Indian communities that populated Rama and the surrounding countryside. It struck me as slightly strange that he still seemed so much an outsider in the way he talked about his parishioners, despite his long years living among them.

He spoke about the literacy campaign around 1980, and the number of Cuban teachers who had come as part of that crusade. Many of them were killed by the Contras in the early part of their campaign. 'You have to understand that the Cubans were not welcome here. People were suspicious of them. They knew they were putting themselves in danger of being killed.' As we talked on, I asked him about the vaccinations against infectious diseases, and whether these had made a big difference to the life expectancy of the children in this region. His congregation did not like the idea of having their children injected, he said: 'they believe that the Sandinistas will inject them with serum that will make them forget God'. I asked him had he tried to dispel this superstition. 'Yes', he smiled, 'but it does seem to persist'.

This priest seemed to represent a very traditional form of missionary work. His job was the spreading of the gospel, and he was not going to get involved in political debate with his parishioners about practical matters. Maybe he had learnt a political reluctance during the Somoza period, or perhaps he was reflecting the wariness of his own parishioners. Possibly he was implacably opposed to the Sandinista government, and was waiting for a good time to express that opposition. I found it impossible to be sure.

Certainly he represented a different strand of thinking within the church from the many priests I heard about in the northern regions who were active in the implementation of the health and education programmes of the new government. These priests have been prime targets for the Contras, and two of Nicaragua's most loved martyrs are a couple of lay catechists who, despite torture, refused to betray their community or denounce the Sandinista Front. They were horribly mutilated in front of one another, and finally killed. Mary Hartmann, an American Maryknoll sister who has been working in Nicaragua for nearly 27 years, represents this tradition well. She now works full-time for the National Commission for the Promotion and Protection of Human Rights in Nicaragua, and sees the ending of Contra violence as the most important aim for Christians in Nicaragua. She is a gaunt woman, with an appearance of long-term ill health, but her energy is unstoppable. She travels to the most dangerous regions of the country regularly, and is visibly affected as she tells of the violence against children and unarmed villagers. She reserves a huge well of anger for the US government for financing and backing these atrocities. I was lucky enough to meet her several times, either alone or with other journalists. She always found the time and space to give detailed briefings about new human rights violations by the Contras. And she spoke with such passion on behalf of a people she sees as her own.

Mary Hartmann came to Nicaragua as a US missionary in the time of Somoza. Then she encountered real fear of the government in her congregations. She reiterated a point made to me by Nicaraguan women about the fear of rape by members of the hated 'Guardia' at that time. It was a common occurrence, and something which happened frequently to young teenage girls or to women in an advanced state of pregnancy. The only parallel she can see to the fear that people lived under in those days is the current fear of the Contras. When they come into a remote village which has no protection from the Sandinista army, people are scared out of their wits, awaiting the inevitable killing, torture and burning of houses which accompanies such attacks. Many of the Contras are ex-Guardia members, so their violence and contempt for the ordinary people does not surprise Mary Hartmann. She was one of the most impressive people I have ever met. Quiet and unassuming, with no trace of ego, her Christianity meant working ceaselessly, and always mustering some energy to contribute something more to the information sought by visitors from outside. 'If we can just help the world to know the horrors being carried out in the name of the US government, then our office here will be worthwhile', she told me.

Although divisions continue within the church, matters have improved greatly in church-state relations since the appointment of a new papal nuncio in 1986. There have been regular meetings between the church and government to exchange views on the Constitution, on the peace process, and on education. While there is not always agreement on these issues, there has been less public posturing by the church in opposition to the Nicaraguan government, and an approach of peaceful coexistence now seems to operate. The Sandinistas, encouraged by this improved attitude, made the generous gesture of appointing their long-time critic, Obando Y Bravo, as mediator in the crucial peace talks with the Contras. This was a significant gesture towards the tens of thousands of Nicaraguans who might disagree with Obando's politics, but who nevertheless see him as their spiritual leader.

Before appointing Cardinal Obando as mediator, in January 1988, the government had also chosen him from a panel of three bishops proposed by the hierarchy to head the National Commission for Reconciliation, which each Central American country was required to establish under the terms of the Central American Peace Plan. Controversy has sprung up around the Cardinal again, however, as he is accused of having squandered one million dollars out of four million, given by the US for verifying the ceasefire of March 1988. Apparently he had bought a dozen luxury jeeps with some of the money, and had done very little verification. This has led to bad publicity for him, even in the US. It should also be mentioned, in view of the huge international profile of Obando Y Bravo, that the Contras always refer to him as 'our Bishop', and that his first stop after being made Cardinal in Rome was to say mass in Miami, with Contra leaders present. The church is not only a part of Nicaraguan life, it reflects its contradictions and hostilities faithfully.

In all of this, Nicaragua is still a predominantly peasant society, with forms of religious devotion common to such societies. Marianism is predominant in many Latin American cultures. Nicaraguans explain their particular devotion to Mary by saying that she is their approachable patron saint, and that she intercedes for them with God. This devotion to Mary is celebrated in a novena lasting from November 28th to December 6th, leading up to the celebration of the feast of the Immaculate Conception. The Purisima, as it is known, is a huge feast in Nicaragua. It is also an essentially female religious ceremony organised, led and carried out by women. And it's something they take great pride in.

I was invited to a Purisima ceremony by a Nicaraguan woman I knew, in her local barrio of Bello Horizonte, a working-class suburb of Managua. Rows of long wooden benches were lined up in front of an altar in the street, with a small statue of the virgin, and hundreds of flowers, cards and rosary beads. One of the local women read out the prayers to the assembled congregation, mainly women and children. Then there were hymns and more readings of prayers. When the prayers ended, the men, who had been in the background, started a fireworks display to the huge excitement of the children. The prayers and chanting go on each night for nine nights, and women pray for intentions and for assistance granted over the year. On 8    December, the Purisima itself, people visit each other in their homes, and the children receive gifts of small presents, sweets and fruits.

In the past, the Purisima could be a time of great social pressure on parents to provide a 'good' celebration in their homes. Now the orientation is towards the local community. People who have some money contribute towards fairy lights, fireworks and flowers for the altar for the whole street. The celebration is a public one, with a strong feeling of local involvement. In addition, the Nicaraguan government distributes small presents and toys to children in the Plaza de la Revolucion, so no child goes without a plaything because of poverty. The Purisima reflects the spontaneous and community nature of much of Nicaraguan religion. It is a novena which is not sponsored or pushed in any way by the institutional church. Priests do not lead the celebrations, they are led by local women. It is an indicator of how deeply held people's religious beliefs are. On another level it demonstrates the inordinate ability of Nicaraguans (and Nicaraguan women in particular) to enjoy themselves with very little. After the prayers, the beakers of fruit juice, the handful of candies, and the excitement on a child's face watching the fireworks, make the daily interminable struggle to survive bearable for another while.

Nicaragua is a fervently religious country, yet people are not sheep-like in their religiosity. They continue to live their lives, often in contradiction to the teachings of their church. When the Pope on his visit to Nicaragua chided the Sandinista priests, but refused to condemn Contra violence, people indicated their sense of betrayal by chanting 'We want peace'. In everyday life too, there are difficult choices.

People want divorce and contraception, and they now have them, despite the Church's opposition. Thousands of Nicaraguan women every year have abortions despite the teaching of their church on the matter. While people do not always keep all the commandments of their church, they have a trust that God, who has seen them through so much struggle, will look with kindness on them at the end of the day.

Kate Hughes

Many of those disabled in the war are very young. Here they participate in a march to highlight their plight.

# Plenty to Sing About

It was a few days before the rains came. The dryness had built up over the previous three months and now it was a parching searing heat. It was almost too hot to move. I was amazed that Nicaraguans at this stage of the year felt the heat as much as I did myself. Things were quieter than usual. In the evenings people sat fanning themselves or drinking 'frescos'. The evening calm was accompanied by the constant buzz of crickets. Even they sounded as though they were fanning themselves ferociously with their wings. 'The evening sounds of music and dancing will be back in a few days', said Anna, 'even if the rains don't come. We don't like to sit still too long'.

She was right. There is a vibrant and busy feel to Nicaraguan culture. The following Saturday night we were wading through inches of warm rainwater. Our destination was an open thatched hall, where five bands queued up to entertain the populace. People clapped and danced, and sang along. 'We feel now that we have plenty to sing about', said Anna. 'Hope is a great inspiration to all our musicians and artists. Even when there are no guitars, we have our dreams to sing about. And we know the guitars will come.'

Cultural activity is affected by the shortages. Musical instruments, oil paints, make-up and costumes for the theatre, are all in short supply. Yet there is a great sense of cultural renaissance. Music is playing all the time. In the streets and pubs, it's mariachi and salsa. In the bigger settings it's steel bands and discos. In the centre run by the Nicaraguan cultural workers' union, it's jazz and classical music. They all seem to find an audience. During my stay in

Bluefields, on the Atlantic coast, the reggae beat accompanied dancers as they rehearsed in the streets for a local dancing festival.

The murals on the gables of walls devastated by the earthquake are symbolic as well as colourful. Out of defeat can come optimism. You see them all over Managua and the other large towns, painted by artists working with the local communities. They depict, in vivid colours, the struggle for freedom, with many blood-spattered stars and stripes, the faces of Sandino and Fonseca, the familiar coffee bushes and their busy pickers, a woman carrying her baby and a rifle, and some more abstract representations of the new life. They cheer up an urban landscape that would otherwise be run down and dusty. People use the freedom that is now theirs to make their mark on walls and open spaces. And the impact is strong.

But it is in the realm of theatre that the sharpest debates on Nicaraguan culture have emerged. The Association of Sandinista Cultural Workers (the ASTC or cultural trade union) has argued for taking up the Western 'classics' and adapting them for Nicaraguan consumption. The opposite school of thought is led by Alan Bolt, certainly the country's foremost writer and theatre director. Bolt comes from a wealthy background on Nicaragua's Atlantic Coast, but he has put all his resources, material and literary, into making real his dream of a culture based on the myths and stories of Nicaragua's Indian past, and its changing reality today. 'Here, we are a long way from your James Joyce', he said as we sat on the verandah outside his purpose-built campesino theatre and home. 'Our stories are our own.'

The most basic cultural discussion for socialists is often about 'high' and 'low' art, and how revolutionary artists can expropriate the best of bourgeois cultural tradition while making it accessible and interesting to the majority of the people. The cultural life of the poor has never been a matter of much artistic interest, because art has been about the exchange of exclusive commodities (e.g. paintings) and honouring the owning classes in society. Aristocratic patronage of classical art, from music to theatre, set an agenda of what was uplifting and worthwhile as culture. In this century Hollywood put a blatantly commercial and often political pressure on film-makers to produce an acceptable version of life, and talented artists have sometimes baulked openly at what they are expected to make of the freer literature and scripts they started off with. This is not to say that nothing great has ever been achieved within the system of bourgeois culture. But Nicaragua, as a revolutionary changing society, needed to do something more to redress the new relationships between its people. I'm reminded of the scene in John Arden and Margaretta D'Arcy's *Little Grey Home in the West* where a family are being evicted from their home. The sister is chided for becoming friendly with the film maker who is over to 'cover the event'. She defends him by saying, 'But he is an artist', to which the reply is; 'Confront him with the situation we are in; put his wonderful artistry to some test of the truth'.[1]

Nicaragua is a small country, trying to change its social and economic relations in a hostile world. For Alan Bolt this is crucial. All of the works considered to be great works of art came from the metropolitan heartland of colonialism. It is not that Britain, France, Germany and the United States produced more talented individuals than countries like Peru, Kenya, Pakistan or Nicaragua, but that their concerns became the epitome of human concern. Cultural colonialism meant that the peoples of underdeveloped and peasant countries had their experience denied its importance. What was culturally significant in global terms was what appealed to the Austrian Emperor or to John F. Kennedy. (Talking to Alan Bolt, I was reminded of similar points made by feminists about the exclusion of female experience from history, and how great Irish writers have been adopted and passed off by the British as British).

What Bolt and his campesino theatre are trying to do is to draw on popular folk memory and rituals to create a new art form, one that is full of colour and allegory, but that is accessible and familiar to ordinary peasant communities. On the land of his own house, near Matagalpa, they have built a large semi-open theatre space which is used for rehearsal and performance. Nearby is the living space for the company, who come and spend the whole period of rehearsal there, completely involved in the creation and improvisation of their work. They also farm the land, fence in orchards, and use open-air toilets from which the waste is recycled as land fertiliser. Most of the buildings are made from bamboo cane, an ecologically sound timber which can grow again in a few years, as opposed to the hundreds of years it takes to replace one hardwood tree.

They plan to develop a new culture, taking the more familiar Hispanic influences and reworking them with the culture and stories of the indigenous Indians. In this way a culture specific to the mestizo, or mixed race, background of Nicaragua will evolve. Bolt and his company are involved in a heated debate with the ASTC, the Cultural Workers Union, and the Ministry of Culture around these questions. These want to take 'great' works of art and put them on in Nicaragua. They stress the importance of high quality in the artist, and are anxious to have visitors from other countries expound their native classics in Nicaragua.

There was a very different feeling about Alan Bolt's theatre. I arrived at a good time. A group of peasants had just arrived from the Rio San Juan region, an area in the remote southern war zone. They had been working on some theatrical ideas with Bolt's company and they had arrived to see the company in action and to develop further their collaboration. The campesinos were mainly elderly, with weatherbeaten lines of hardship engrained on their faces. The play they were working on was tied to their hope of getting a dam for their area, and they discussed what they could do with a dam, and how the hardship without one could be portrayed on stage. The women were very interested in a play that had come out of one of the other campesino theatres, dealing with how women's ideas are not taken seriously in a rural community. Even the older women were vociferous in pointing out examples of how they had been ignored in the past, only to be proved right by events. The discussion was lively.

After the meeting, Alan Bolt's company performed. It was a comedy piece based on an old Indian myth, about a young man going to ask a woman's hand in marriage from her father, and the obstacles put in his way. Throughout, humour was derived from the macho pretence at self-confidence, and eventually the marriage happens because the daughter herself decides in his favour. It wasn't exactly advanced feminism, but because the story it was based on was so familiar to the audience it met with great hilarity.

Involvement by ordinary people seems to be a keystone in much of Nicaragua's culture. I saw a film made in the north of the country called 'Mujeres de la Frontena', 'Women of the Front'. It dealt with the lives of women on a large agricultural co-operative, while their husbands and brothers were away at war. The women, doing jobs which were pretty new to them, were soon running a model farm and negotiating with the Ministry of Agriculture to introduce tractors. However, as soon as this was agreed and the woman who had played a key role in developing the farm was set to travel to Managua to receive them, the men arrived back from the front, and demanded that their representative should go instead. The film was about the debate that followed, about the relationships that ensued when the tractors arrived, with certain men taking the position that they would not talk to any woman who drove a tractor. In the end, perhaps inevitably, they came round. What was most interesting was that most of the parts were played by real agricultural workers, wearing their own clothes, and you could see them getting huge enjoyment out of the debates on screen. I read an interview with the director of the film and she described the difficulty she had had in talking the campesinos out of wearing their Sunday best while tilling the fields in the film. Perhaps under-standably, for their first time on film, they wanted to look their best, rather than just authentic. This was the first full length feature film made in Nicaragua, by Nicaraguans.

Nicaragua's Hispanic culture is exemplified in the popularity of a national form of bull-fighting, the bull-bait. Somewhat reluctantly, I dragged myself along to a bull-bait in Diriamba. We sat in stalls around the dusty arena, while a hugely out of tune brass band struck up. Its gusto compen-sated for the lack of tone. Then out came a dozen or so docile-looking oxen. The men in the ring, many of whom were already very drunk, rushed around pulling the bulls by the tail, throwing sand in their eyes, and generally trying to torment them. The one ox who voiced a minor objection to this treatment was singled out with a lasso and the rest left the ring. The lasso was tightened around his neck until he started to splutter and choke. While he lay up against a tree trunk trying to get his breath, a leather belt with stirrups was fastened around his waist. A young boy of about fifteen climbed up on him, and the bull was released. He was by this stage very angry and used his new-found freedom to try to gore the boy on his back, or at least to throw him off. Meanwhile the 'matadors' ran around with red cloths attempting to distract him. All the time the terrified animal pissed on the ground as though he was wondering what new horror was about to befall him. It was animal-baiting in the raw, without the supposed glamour of the costumes of the Spanish bull-fight. But it was hugely popular. Its one advantage was that eventually the bull was released, with his life, if not his demeanour, intact. Later that particular week I read that one of the 'matadors' at the same arena was killed by a bull, gored in the jugular vein. Although bull-baiting is not as dangerous as bull-fighting, there is minimal training involved for the volunteer matadors. This aspect of the Spanish cultural legacy left me completely cold, even with the cheering and music still ringing in my ears. Bull-baiting is considered an occasion of great festivity, and usually takes place at the same time as the celebration of local saints, as on that day in Diriamba. Religious feasts are celebrated uproariously, with a lot of drinking and merry making, and even beauty contests.

Poetry forms a central part of Nicaragua's cultural tradition. From Ruben Dario through Leonel Rugama to Ernesto Cardenal, Minister for Culture today, poetry has been used to express thoughts, both rebellious and romantic, which would otherwise have been silent. The island of Solentiname, where the 'fishermen-farmers-poets-fighters' of Nicaragua based themselves from 1970, became a haven for Sandinista thought and organisation. The community was founded by Fernando Cardenal, Sandinista priest and now Minister for Education, and it became famous for its poetry workshops, arts and crafts, and the 'primitive' style of painting now common in Nicaraguan posters and paintings. It has remained a community loyal to the Sandinista government, perhaps because it sees the profound change in life possible under the new regime. In the 1984 election Solentiname recorded the highest national vote for the FSLN, ninety-five per cent.

To rebel and to reveal oneself are the twin aims of Giaconda Belli's poetry, as her colleague Jose Coronel Urtecho said in introducing her book *Sobre la Grama (On the Grass)* in February 1974.[2] Belli is the most loved of today's Nicaraguan poets, and her work is very beautifully direct, and true to experience. Some of her poems have a directly political ring to them, such as 'Those who bear dreams', a tribute to her comrades in political struggle:

> worlds of brothers and sisters,
> of men and women who called each other companeros,
> who taught each other to read,
> consoled each other in times of death,
> healed and cared for each other,
> loved and helped each other
> in the art of loving and in the defence of happiness.

Giaconda Belli came from a well-to-do family in Nicaragua. She married a wealthy man, and had on the surface a perfect life, with every comfort she could want. In her own words: 'But there came a time when I began feeling an intense contradiction between the life I was leading and what I saw going on around me. I noticed these contradictions first of all because my Christian upbringing made such injustice intolerable to me, and secondly because my family were traditional Conservatives and anti-Somoza. And I grew up in an atmosphere of opposition to the regime. But I could never see a way out. I didn't know what I might do. All I knew was that I couldn't go on living the kind of life I was living.'[3]

In 1969 she became involved with the Frente Sandinista and worked with them over the next six years, raising her own consciousness and doing practical work. It was around this time that she began writing poetry, out of the female experience of life, love, politics, and motherhood. Her work was very open in its dealing with female sexuality, which did not always meet with popular approval. As she put it herself: 'I was singing out of my pleasure at being alive, of feeling glad to be a woman and living in a time when things were happening which promised such important changes. I was also rebelling against the hypocrisy of society. Because at first I spoke very innocently of the things I was feeling I saw nothing wrong with talking about my body or about such beautiful and daily things as making love. Men had been writing about those things for centuries. But it became scandalous that a well-bred girl . . . would use words like belly, breast, and so on'.

In 1975 Belli's political involvement led to her being condemned *in absentia* by a court martial, and she was forced to leave the country. During her exile in Mexico, a period she looks back on with great sadness, she wrote *Linea de Fuego*, which won her the Casa de la Americas poetry prize. After that she was internationally established. She returned to Nicaragua in 1979, to witness the start of the new Nicaragua. She feels that real revolution has to be about total change, and that it is during peacetime that the really hard work must begin. 'It's a search for . . . the revolution from the inside out, the search for one's authentic identity, for new human relations which are difficult because one knows that it's necessary to destroy much of the past, but we don't really know what we're going to replace it with. I'm talking about the more intimate level — the traditional man-woman relations, for example.'

One of the secrets of her writing is the honesty of her descriptions of sexual wonder, pleasure in the art of love-making, without the shadows of guilt common to cultures imbued with Catholicism. In her poem, 'Brief Lessons in Eroticism', she tells the reader:

Go over the entire length many times,
Find the lake with the white water lilies,
Caress the lily's center with your anchor
Plunge deep drown yourself stretch your limbs
Don't deny yourself the smell the salt the sugar
The heavy winds cumulonimbus-lungs
The brain's dense fog
Earthquake of legs
Sleeping tidal wave of kisses.

I love the immediate warmth of her writing, which gives a real sense of a vibrant and fulfilled womanhood. This is true whether she is writing about sexuality, motherhood or politics.

Poetry can create a bridge between the here and now of reality and the dream of what could be. In this the very essence of poetry is revolutionary, because it demonstrates what humanity can aspire to without the dull ache of the means of achieving those aspirations, the committee rooms, the debates, the fighting. Belli's poem, 'Let's Draw', sums up for me an atmosphere I saw all over Nicaragua, an excitement about the future:

Let's listen
Let's draw the future in the sand
and men and women drawing
a world with no divisions
and a blue world where the sky isn't compartmentalised
where love might leave the beds and the parks
and enter the bedrooms, the mops, the bundles of clothes,
the raw vegetables, the pots, and the children.
Let's draw a man and woman engaged in conversation
accompanying each other with their eyes beyond the
    door
A man and a woman happily walking on the sidewalks
    on Sundays
as if they had been born together.
Let's draw a single world where even small things are
    important.
Let's draw a home that's the same size as the factory

131

the same size as the best, most valiant battle.
Let's draw love with big letters;
and men and women loving each other
let's draw them like the angular stone of a beautiful
   building.
Let's draw the strength of a man and a woman
and their love like that of lions for their cubs
Let's draw a star of light
a bright star on the man's forehead
a bright star on the woman's.
Let's draw ourselves with the colours we love most
the colour of peace
the colour of tomorrow
the swaying colour of sugarcane
the colour of that house that we call my house
Let's draw ourselves
like two hurricanes that hold hands
and draw the world over again.[4]

To say Nicaraguans get great joy from poetry, music and
dancing is a cliché, but a true one. No matter how poor the
circumstances people were living in, they made a cultural
outlet for themselves, a Saturday night party, a children's
get together, a bop by the sea. On the coffee farm I worked
on there were only a couple of guitars, but this didn't stop
people from making their own impact; the guitars were
passed around although formally owned by one of the
musicians, unaccompanied singing was hugely popular, and
people made up pan pipes and percussive instruments from
the bamboo and trees around them.

   There are two distinct cultures in Nicaragua, the Spanish
colonial heritage of the western seaboard, and the British/
Caribbean legacy on the eastern Atlantic coast. The cultural
differences, tied in with political and economic dichotomy
over the years, have led to demands for autonomy on the
east coast in the period since 1979. It is here that the Miskito
Indians, the Sumu and Rama peoples, and Nicaragua's black
population, live. It is an area that is rich in natural resources,
but one that has been consistently underdeveloped over the
centuries. The fact that the 'Costenos' were sea traders was

used as an excuse not to build roads in the region. Raw materials were taken from the mines but money was not put in to the mining towns, and the population of the Atlantic coast was severely under-represented in Somoza's parliament. The separate languages and culture of the region were ignored, and all schooling was through Spanish, although local children did not speak it. The stories and crafts of the Atlantic coast were ignored and attempts made to supplant them with the Hispanic culture and ways of the West coast. All of this led to a suspicion of central government, a suspicion that is still held about the Sandinistas.

When I travelled to Bluefields, I used the route travelled by most local people. I hitchhiked as far as Rama in the centre of the country, and from there took the boat to the East coast's capital. I got a lift most of the way to Rama in a military truck, which was great, because its size and construction shielded me from most of the lumps and bumps of the potholed roads. On the last part of the road journey I encountered the greatest difficulty I ever had hitching in Nicaragua. The reason of course, is that there are Contra camps in the jungle surrounding the area, and any local farmer giving a lift to an internationalista (who are generally considered to be supportive of the Nicaraguan government) would leave himself open to attack. However, I got there eventually.

Rama is like an old American frontier town, and that's basically what it is. Its main occupation is trading and transportation between the east and west coasts. There are two hotels, one of which has rats, I'm told. The other hotel, overlooking the boat and the river to Bluefields, has a saloon bar in its reception, from where the locals eye strangers with scepticism. The rooms upstairs should be picturesque, but there are no windows overlooking the water. The only place the river can be seen from is the wooden constructions that serve as bathrooms. You can gaze downstream as you shower.

I was itching to get on the boat by the time the next morning came. As we all stood waiting to board, we had to watch while the cargo from Bluefields was unloaded and the provisions for the coast for that day were packed on. This happens every day, laboriously by hand, and takes several hours. The boat journey itself takes six to eight hours, which are long in the baking heat with no cover. On board there was a young girl, no more than fifteen years of age, with a tiny baby of a few weeks old. She spent the whole journey trying to find ways of shielding the child from the scorching rays of the sun. I was reminded that many small babies in Nicaragua who die do so because of dehydration, from the burning heat.

On the boat journey, I became aware that I was travelling into a different culture. People spoke English, in the jive talk rhythms of the Caribbean. There was a more easy-going attitude to life and politics (not at all the same commitment to the new process as on the Pacific coast), and a large emphasis on music and chant. Of course these are superficial observations, but when you have eight hours to sit on a boat with people you get a certain sense of what they are about.

The historic suspicion of the Managuan governments has been carried over to the present day. The people of the Atlantic coast regard Pacific Nicaraguans as 'Spanish' and the Sandinistas were just another foreign government to them. The Miskito Indians were a prime recruiting ground for the Contras in the early 1980s; living as they did around the Rio Coco near the northern border with Honduras, they were often pressured into fighting. Others joined with enthusiasm, hoping for a better deal for themselves and their people if the Sandinistas were overthrown. They believed that their religion (the Moravian church) was about to be suppressed and they saw no evidence of a recognition of their separate identity, in terms of language or culture. The Nicaraguan government made serious errors in the early period, including the forced resettlement of some Miskitos further south and inland, away from their beloved Rio Coco, a river with a particular mystical significance, where they had fished and worshipped for centuries.

There is a recognition now that this was a mistaken policy. Tomas Borge has spearheaded a process of autonomy for the Atlantic coast, with a regional parliament, re-investment of local profits in the region and a recognition of its cultural distinction. The local languages are being supported, and bi-lingualism has been introduced in education; the Caribbean and Indian cultures are being encouraged and funded. This has not led to an overnight conversion to Sandinismo, as Amelia Dixon Cunningham of the Nicaraguan Autonomy Commission told me. 'There is real suspicion and it goes back a long time. It wasn't helped by what the government did in its early years in power. But the people of the Atlantic Coast are beginning to see, very slowly, that this government does want to help.' She told me that when she first went to Managua to work on the autonomy project with the government, she was completely snubbed by her own people, who thought she was a traitor. But she believed that the Sandinistas would give the coast its autonomy, if they could only hear why and what the people wanted. Now, six years on, her work has paid off. The vast majority of the Indians who were fighting on the Contra side have laid down their arms and come home, accepting the government amnesty for former Contras, and becoming involved in the autonomy process.

The recognition of the diverse cultures of the Atlantic and Pacific coasts was one task. Another was the popularisation of the already strong literary and artistic tradition. There has been a flourishing of community theatre, wall murals, mask-making, crafts and pottery, street music, poster screening and open poetry readings. Although there has not been much money to support individual artists, the Ministry of Culture is involved in cultural activities all over Nicaragua. One such event I attended was a campesino music festival in Matagalpa, which was reminiscent of many an Irish fleadh. The difference was colour. Each group of players had woven jackets in the bright Indian shades of fuchsia, jade, orange, blue and yellow. The field where the festival took place was a blaze of festive colour and excitement. The United States has had a huge cultural impact on Nicaragua. Baseball is the national sport, followed by basketball. Everyone loves T-shirts with messages in English, and baseball hats are worn daily by Nicaraguan men, including Daniel Ortega. American pop singers like

Madonna, Michael Jackson and Lionel Ritchie are hugely popular, and the government has been making efforts to 'rescue' the inherently Nicaraguan aspects of culture through its support for local festivals, art and music.

Ernesto Cardenal, Nicaragua's Minister for Culture, pointed out the important role of culture as an expression of the change in how people were thinking when he met members of the first Irish coffee brigade. 'A great culture existed, strong, particularly the literary tradition', he said. 'This was very important in the revolution. Also there has always been a great tradition of music and protest songs, as expressions of anti imperialism. Many writers and painters were involved in the struggle. Many died, were tortured, exiled. Our culture was already in place and it really blossomed with the triumph of the revolution — the culture was popularised, it now belongs to the people, not to an elite group.'

1. *The Little Grey Home in the West,* Margaretta D'Arcy and John Arden, Pluto Press 1982, Page 56.
2. *Envio,* May 1988, 'Women, Poetry, New Nicaraguan Culture'. The quotes from Giaconda Belli's poetry all come from this excellent article.
3. *Risking a Somersault in the Air—Conversations with Nicaraguan Writers,* by Margaret Randall, Solidarity Publications, San Francisco, 1984.
4. Translations by Steven F. White for *From Eve's Rib,* a book of Giaconda Belli's selected poems, to be published in the US by Curbstone Press, 321 Jackson St., Willimantic, CT 06226.

# Ireland and Nicaragua

Our empirical and oral traditions lead to great temptations to make neat comparisons with Ireland when we travel abroad. It would be very false to draw formal parallels between the situation in Nicaragua and that in Ireland. The most fundamental fact of life there is underdevelopment, a poverty shocking to Western eyes. This is basic, and makes the advances in health and education stand out in a country suffering so much lack of wealth. Once this is understood, it is possible to draw comparisons, to see points in common, in our histories, personalities, our ways of organising, our devotion to Catholicism, our cultures, our treatment of women. For these purposes I have drawn on the experience and views of some activists in the Nicaraguan solidarity movement here, to see what lessons we can learn from Nicaragua's struggle.

Irish political life has been dominated over the last few centuries by our relationship with Britain and a desire to win national independence. Our political structures, land ownership, education and language were all decided by an imperial parliament which established its rule here hundreds of years ago. Nicaragua suffered the same intervention; the Spanish arrived five hundred years ago, followed by the British on the Atlantic coast in the eighteenth century. In 1821 Spain recognised Nicaragua's independence by treaty signed in Madrid. Just ten years later Britain recognised the sovereignty of the Atlantic coast. It could be argued that both powers had taken what they wanted in terms of raw materials and precious ores by that period, and were content to allow a formal independence in which they could continue to prosper and trade. Yet it was just after this period, in the second half of the last century, that American intervention began, with the journeys of William Walker. Yankee troops and marines policed Nicaragua up to their routing by Sandino in the 1930s. After that US intervention was indirect and economic, until the Contra war began to be funded in 1981. The shadow of foreign involvement has been there right through Nicaraguan history.

'Our nearness to the imperialist power is the biggest similarity between Ireland and Nicaragua', says Anne McCluskey, 'it could be said that we are Britain's back yard. It has no regard to our sovereign laws, such as that on extradition, and the United States is doing the same thing in Nicaragua, ignoring their independence. At the same time they are an underdeveloped socialist country while we are an advanced capitalist country. We had hopes of change at the beginning of the century, but James Connolly was defeated where the Sandinistas won.'

Nicaragua achieved a measure of national independence in the last century, but there was a resistance to granting Home Rule to Ireland, which had to settle in 1921 for independence for part of the country. Partition is often a legacy left behind in former British colonies, yet there was no attempt to enforce partition in Nicaragua by making offers to the Miskito people of the Atlantic coast. Nevertheless, there is a somewhat partitionist set of attitudes in eastern Nicaragua, which are easier to work around because they have not been formally instituted as a separate state. The cultural and political differences between the two regions of Nicaragua have been recognised, and the Miskito/Caribbean peoples given an autonomous parliament. This regional parliament is under the overall sovereignty of Nicaragua, yet it has power to look after its own citizens within that national unit. In this way it is hoped that the suspicions that have existed between the different peoples of Nicaragua will start to dissolve, and a true harmony will emerge.

'Both countries had a long oppression', says Sr. Joanna O'Connor. 'For Ireland it was 700 years of Britain, for

Nicaragua, 300 years of Spain. The real problem in Ireland is that when we got our independence there was no social revolution, there was just a change from one government to another. It wasn't a popular revolution. In Nicaragua the whole nation apart from the elite supported the Sandinistas in 1978; even Bishop Obando Y Bravo did. Whereas our leaders only got support when they became martyrs.'

'In Ireland we have not had a very clear philosophy', Sr. Joanna continued. 'In Nicaragua the demand for land for the people was basic, but in Ireland there had been some land reform by the turn of the century. So the extremes between rich and poor were not so extreme.' Clearly, where the polarisation is as stark as it was in Nicaragua in 1978, where real hunger and constant deaths among the poor contrasted with a tiny privileged elite around the Somoza family, it is easier to convince people of the need for radical revolutionary change. Nevertheless, power was not handed to the Sandinistas on a platter. For many years they travelled the country as teachers, bringing their educational skills and discussing the need for political transformation. On the military front they operated as a very successful guerilla band, receiving popular support for actions such as holding members of Somoza's National Assembly hostage in order to get food distributed and political prisoners released. But perhaps the most crucial preparation for national leadership was the successful discussion between the three divergent factions within the Frente Sandinista on a programme for change. The agrarian-based movement, along with the harder line urban Marxists in the party, placed itself behind the third faction, a group of intellectuals in the cities who were forging links with all of the discontented layers in Nicaraguan society. Daniel Ortega was the leader of this faction, and to this day the unity which was agreed as fundamental to success has held. The whole nation was involved in the desire for change and its execution. No radical force in Ireland could command that sort of unity at present.

The base line of poverty which the Sandinistas inherited is something that is hard for us to comprehend. When I came home from Nicaragua I was amazed at how quickly I'd forgotten the difference. Despite the advances outlined in earlier chapters, the hardship is palpable and constant. 'Nicaragua is a country where life is not easy. There are shortages of everything. The last seven years of war have taken a heavy toll in human lives, limbs, emotions and material damage,' says Eadaoin Heussaff, who spent a year living there. 'But despite being battered and severely under-developed, Nicaragua is an important example to other countries, and not only those that are marginalised and deprived of a say in international affairs. Nicaragua's example is that of independence and of a society where *people* are a priority. I believe the Nicaraguan government has made a genuine effort to improve the situation of the majority of Nicaraguans who previously were ignored or exploited. The fact that daily life is so hard in Nicaragua today is not the fault of the government; if the country had not suffered several years of war and economic blockade, its situation would be vastly different today. And despite their loudly expressed unhappiness with the present situation, most Nicaraguans recognise that. In a recent opinion poll 58% of those surveyed gave positive ratings (from fair to excellent) to the government's handling of the economy since it came to power, and 68% gave positive ratings to the government's overall political performance. That is an extraordinary level of approval in a country suffering such a chronic economic crisis, but it indicates the maturity and political consciousness which Nicaraguans have developed in the last ten years.'

The three fundamental principles of the Sandinistas' political philosophy—political pluralism, a mixed economy and a non-aligned foreign policy — are central to the changes happening in Nicaragua today. 'They can be seen to be genuinely held principles, with a real commitment to upholding them,' says Fionnuala Rogerson, 'unlike our own mere lip-service to similar aims. However, it is probably, above all, the poor and marginalised in our society who would gain most had they the opportunity to experience for themselves the new Nicaraguan approach to development, based on the creation of a society where the needs of the poor majority come foremost, where they have a real say in their own future.'

This point is one reiterated by Nicaraguan solidarity activists, and tallies with my own experience there. Although the absolute poverty is much greater in Nicaragua, poor people are not so alienated or unrepresented as they are in Ireland. 'Poor people here have other problems as well as having no money. A homeless person may be alcoholic, because they are homeless', says Anne McCluskey, 'their other ills come from poverty. While we must not romanticise poverty in Nicaragua it is true to say that everyone is on an equal basis, poverty is not shameful, people can talk about it. Here people on the dole have to constantly prove they've been looking for a job or they are threatened with losing their dole. Our confidence and ability to get out of the poverty trap is constantly being undermined. We are told that other nations are better, that emigration is a good thing. Poor people have no pride and dignity.'

Sr. Joanna O'Connor feels that in Ireland the poor have been marginalised and pushed to the edge of society. 'The difference is that 90 per cent of people are poor in Nicaragua, and one-third are here. That third are treated as sub-human beings. Where I'm working we've had a problem with sewage seeping up through the ground. The attitude is, it doesn't matter because you're in St. Teresa's Gardens. People are actually dying because of health cutbacks, and youth services have disappeared in poor areas. The attitude of the system here is careless to the poor, and this is leading to violence and a sense of hopelessness.'

'In Nicaragua, the poor have power, you get that sense in the barrios', Sr. Joanna continues. 'In Ireland they're not represented in government or in local decision-making bodies. Then you have groups like Concerned Parents Against Drugs emerging, taking power to themselves because they're not included in the structures of power. In these areas people don't want to see police, they're completely foreign to them.'

By contrast, popular participation is real in Nicaragua. People go along to voice their views at the 'Face the People' meetings with government ministers and the President himself. Their complaints are broadcast on national radio live, along with the replies, even where these are inadequate. There are popular militias and neighbourhood defence groups in every locality. The unions and farm workers' associations negotiate with individual managements and the state directly. There is a feeling of trying to sort out the worst problems to improve people's basic lives.

Because Nicaragua is such an underdeveloped economy, everybody is involved in the economic process, whether they are laundering clothes, making tractor parts or picking cotton. Yet despite this involvement, the economy is in a dire situation. 'The economic damage suffered by Nicaragua as a direct result of the Contra war is now running at over 1.5 billion dollars,' says Fionnuala Rogerson. '60% of government spending over the past two years has had to be diverted to defence. For some time now there has been absolutely no money available to continue the programmes begun as part of the National Programme for Reconstruction. As a direct result of both the economic and military wars being waged against it, Nicaragua now finds itself in a state of economic crisis. The food supply and distribution system has broken down, the transport system is in chaos, there are constant shortages of electricity, water and petrol, there are major housing shortages, factories have had to close down in order that those producing goods for export which will bring in much-needed foreign currency can remain open'.

In this situation, it is not surprising to find expressed opposition to the government and its policies. This is vocal, and increasing. Commentators state that what the US has failed to do in military terms, it may succeed in doing by an economic war of attrition. My own experience of talking to Nicaraguans left me with the feeling that many of those who gave out loudly about the government and the hardships of their lives were often quite loyal to the Sandinistas when questioned about ousting them. They recognised the problems as being caused by the war, and looked forward to it ending so that they could reap some real benefits from the new system, benefits such as had started to be evident in 1980 before the war. I do not say that this was the situation with all of those who stood in queues berating the government, but there was an ambivalence among many.

Perhaps one striking difference between Ireland and Nicaragua is a feeling that in some way the Sandinistas are seen by the very poorest as representing their interests. In Ireland, the poorest, as represented by the growing numbers of long-term unemployed, do not feel that their interests are articulated in our society. There is no feeling that there is a will to improve their lot when the economic situation changes, that any rising tide will lift *their* boats.

The Catholic church is an important force to be reckoned with, both in Ireland and in Nicaragua. About 90% of both populations subscribe to its beliefs. Yet the Irish church is more monolithic, it is on the right of the world church (as evidenced by the interest paid by the Vatican to the appointment of the successor to Kevin McNamara as Archbishop of Dublin). In Nicaragua the differences evident in the church in the early 1980s show the close involvement of clergy in political debate. 'In Ireland you have a middle-class male church', says Sr Joanna O'Connor. 'It is more concerned with the status quo than with the transformation of Ireland into a society that serves the poor. The 1977 Bishops' Document did not cover their issues, did not touch the ordinary man or woman in the street. Just yesterday there was a death in Mountjoy of a young man from the area I live in. There was no bishop down outside Mountjoy today with his parents and friends.' Sr Joanna is one of those church activists who believes that the silence of the hierarchy lends support to the status quo. She feels that individuals like her do not pose enough of a threat to the dominant church group in Ireland for a real debate to start. Nevertheless she feels that if a social revolution were to happen in Ireland, the church would have to be involved because it is so much a part of our national heritage.

Church members like Sr Joanna O'Connor and the Sisters of Justice see themselves as part of a worldwide movement taking up Vatican Two's 'Option for the Poor'. More commonly known as 'liberation theology', this movement began with a meeting of Latin American clergy back in 1969. They pointed out that 80% of church members were poor, that the church was now the People of God and not the hierarchy, and that they must be served in actions as well as words. Nicaragua has been at the very centre of that movement, whereas here in Ireland it is beginning to happen only very slowly. On the other hand the Irish church has primarily involved itself in moral political issues, allied with the most conservative elements in Irish society. Whether pressuring against free health care for mothers and infants in the 1950s, against contraception in the 1970s, or against divorce and in support of an anti-abortion clause in the Constitution in the 1980s, the church hierarchy has always been opposed to extension of liberal rights, in particular to women. It might be observed that what Irish and Nicaraguan Catholics do have in common is an ability to find an accommodation between their lifestyles and their religiosity. Moral strictures are not universally conformed to, and in the moral area women tend to hold the belief that God will be more understanding of their choices than the institutional church is.

Culturally the two countries are closer than might appear superficially obvious. Although Nicaragua is a third world peasant-based economy, it is not long since most Irish people lived on the land. Certainly our lifestyles have as much in common as we would have with our nearest European neighbours. In both countries there is a strong tradition of music, dance and story-telling. Traditions of group farming, where individuals depend on their neighbours twice a year to complete important work like hay saving, are common to both cultures. Visiting each other's houses is a usual form of social intercourse, there as here. And in the cities, the influences of North American culture, in cinemas and discos, are particularly noticeable among the young. The overall attitude to life in both countries is of an easy-going affability, mixed with a strong dose of fatalism to temper political determination.

Women's lives are very hard in Nicaragua. This is in part due to the poverty, in part due to machismo. There have been improvements in the past ten years, in the areas of child care, equal pay, divorce, sexist advertising, women's legal rights and truly free family planning. Yet attitudes are slow to change and the legislative programme is way in advance of the consciousness of most husbands and fathers. Women holding high political office are still the exceptions, and domestic violence and refusal to recognise paternity of children are still commonplace. Yet there is a strong women's movement, and this reaches to even the most isolated rural pockets. And there are support networks for everything from natural childbirth to alcoholism counselling.

In Ireland, women won a lot of major legal rights in the 1970s. The 1980s have, if anything, been a period of erosion of those rights because of the lack of a strong and vocal women's movement. Women are still organising but in a piecemeal way, on individual issues. As a result of the recession, survival is the keynote. New demands are not being made, and items like equal pay and creche facilities are increasingly reported as luxuries, which can be postponed. Divorce is still illegal, and abortion has had its illegal status underpinned constitutionally. 'The position of women has to be a priority for a changing society, particularly that of poor women,' says Anne McCluskey. 'In Nicaragua there is discussion about machismo, and women's changing role, whereas here, the attitude is "you have your rights, so what are you moaning about?". There's no tolerance of women asking questions. My greatest worry for Nicaraguan women is the fierce hardship they live in. They have to spend such a lot of time queuing, and there's not much power in that.' Sr Joanna feels that in the west the feminist movement is a key tool for the transformation of society, especially if it can address the problems of poor women and get them involved. In Nicaragua, women's priority is the survival of the revolution, because they know that any advances they have made and will make are tied up with that survival.

The tradition of neutrality is strong in Ireland, and most people believe that de Valera's refusal to involve Irish ports in the second world war was his finest hour. In the debate around the Single European Act and since our entry to the European community there has been a widespread suspicion that that neutrality is no longer real. Every vote involving a jont NATO line is watched vigilantly from Ireland to see how independent Ireland's voice remains. Our view of ourselves as European, and as one of The Twelve, certainly colours our attitude to foreign policy. There was surprise when Charles Haughey, the Irish Prime Minister, distanced Ireland from Britain's involvement in the Falklands/Malvinas war, after the sinking of the Belgrano. It is expected that whereas we are not actually involved in any military alliance with Europe, we are not expected to cause embarrassment by raising our voices too loudly in opposition to NATO policy.

borne out by Nicaragua's experience. It has attempted to maintain a non-aligned profile, trading with the capitalist West, the socialist East and the underdeveloped South. Yet the Ortega government's political independence aroused the ire of the Reagan administration as far back as 1983. 'Pressure was being brought to bear by the United States through blocking of loans and other economic sanctions,' says Fionnuala Rogerson. 'In 1983 the US cut its sugar quota by 90% and voted against a 34 million dollars Inter-American Development Bank loan intended to revitalise the fishing industry. Again, in January 1985, another IADB loan, this time 150 million dollars for boosting basic food production, was blocked. Since then the economic war has increased, with further major loans and aid donations being blocked and with the trade embargo of 1985, which has had drastic consequences.'

Yet Fionnuala is hopeful that Irish governments can be pressured into giving some support to Nicaragua, 'despite the fact that in the early 1980s when Ireland was a member of nearly always aligned with the European Community, and never prepared to openly condemn the US'. She points to the fact that in the early '80s when Ireland was a member of the UN security council, we supported Nicaragua on several occasions, and our Ambassador of the time, Noel Dorr, developed a good personal relationship with Nicaragua's Foreign Minister, Miquel D'Escoto. Ray Hooker, chairman of Nicaragua's National Assembly, told activists in Dublin recently of how, when he was addressing the European

Parliament a few years ago, he was under sustained attack from the right. He groaned when he saw another member on the right of the chamber stand up, and prepared himself for the worst. To his surprise, the member spoke in strong defence of Nicaragua and its achievements. It was Fianna Fáil TD Niall Andrews. Fionnuala Rogerson feels that these examples show the importance of pressurising Irish representatives abroad to keep informed on Nicaraguan politics, to enable them to take a genuinely independent stance.

People throughout the world have been inspired by the humanist socialism inherent in the Nicaraguan model. They have been distressed by the war against it, both because people like to see a small country respected, and because they have seen images of the civilian casualties of that war. To me the memory of three tiny children's faces lying in their white coffins, faces bruised and bloodied by the mortar shells that hit them, remains. They are the strongest argument for a peaceful end to the war.

But for Ireland, and people who look to Nicaragua as an example of a new society, what lessons can be learnt from its experience? Anne McCluskey sees working for political change in Ireland as of paramount importance. Otherwise we are not doing enough for Nicaragua, she says. It is impossible to get a real political commitment from TDs in the right wing setup that exists in this country. Sr Joanna O'Connor feels that change must come about in Ireland, but that it must come from the bottom up, with poor people themselves taking up their own issues.

Eadaoin Heussaff also feels there are important lessons to be drawn for Ireland; 'Nicaragua is a country where you can still find a lot of idealism, along with resolute determination. The severe difficulties of the last few years haven't succeeded in destroying that. That kind of idealism is something I feel we lack here. Rather than shrugging our shoulders at the problems and injustices which exist here we could take a lesson from Nicaragua and work actively to create a better society, both in the Republic and in the six counties. I think we could also learn from Nicaragua in terms of political courage. For a long time we've been afraid to assert our independence and choose a path suited to *our* needs i.e. the needs of all Irish citizens, not just some of them. We haven't tried to find out if real nationalism (i.e. putting our own people first) would benefit us more than submitting to the rules laid down by England, Europe and the US.'[1]

For me personally, Nicaragua represents the triumph of commitment over cynicism. I only have to cast my mind back to feel the heat of the midday sun and hear the street vendors calling out the names of those welcome fruits; mandarina, guava, tamarindo. I see the people in the war zones, surrounded by devastation after a Contra attack, quietly beginning to rebuild their homes. I remember the fearless arguing and gesticulating at the president's open meetings with the people. And I look back to one place that indicates what Nicaragua could be, if it were free of war and debt. That was the volcanic lake, Xiloa, near Managua, which has been turned into a people's park in recent years. Thatched dressing-rooms and picnic areas with landscaped shrubs and trees make a beautiful setting for Sundays out. Families throng there, the women swimming in their ordinary clothes, because swimming costumes would be unaffordable luxuries. In that oasis they can forget the harshness of the week. My strongest image of Nicaragua, now that I have been some time back in Ireland, is of the laughter, the singing and the pyramid games played in the water at Xiloa. I think the Nicaraguans I met would be glad that this is what stood out. In the words of Giaconda Belli:

> 'Let's draw ourselves with the colours we love most
> the colour of peace
> the colour of tomorrow
> the swaying colour of sugarcane
> the colour of that house that we call my house.
> Let's draw ourselves
> like two hurricanes that hold hands
> and draw the world over again.'[2]

1. Fionnuala Rogerson, Eadaoin Heussaff and Anne McCluskey are members of the Irish Nicaraguan Support Group. Sr Joanna O'Connor is a member of the Sisters for Justice.
2. *From Eve's Rib,* by Giaconda Belli, translated by Steven White.

# Epilogue

I returned home from Nicaragua in May 1987, and since then elements of the situation have changed, while others have sadly stayed the same. The biggest breakthrough was the signing of the Esquipulas II Accords on 7 August, 1987, when the Central American countries committed themselves to search for a political solution to the problems of the region, without outside interference. Of course making such a pledge, and implementing it, in the sensitive political climate of Central America, are two very different things. And the Accords, while being welcomed initially by the United States, have not fitted into their strategy for the region. So what has been achieved so far, and what are the major hurdles?

The most important development achieved by the Central American Peace Plan has been the coming together of the presidents of Central America to attempt to resolve the crises in their own countries (ie Guatemala, El Salvador, Honduras, Nicaragua and Costa Rica). They focused on the issues of National Dialogue, Amnesty, Ceasefire with opposing troops, and an ending of aid from outside to such irregular forces. In addition it was agreed that no country would allow its territory to be used for aggression against other states in the region. An International Commission on Verification and Follow Up (CIVS) was established, and it consisted of the Ministers of Foreign Affairs of the Central American Countries, of the Contadora Group and the Support Group, and of the Secretaries General (or their representatives) of the Organisation of American States and the United Nations.

Although efforts have been made by the various Central American governments to make some movements towards peace some difficulties have arisen:

— In Guatemala, the government's room to manoeuvre has been very limited, with constant army pressure against moves towards democratisation. The repression against Indian villages continues, and there is no negotiation with the guerilla organisation.

— In El Salvador, the forces of the left were excluded from the national dialogue, and eight of the parties participating in the discussions withdrew after only four months. A small number of FMLN guerillas were released under an amnesty, but no serious ceasefire discussions have been attempted. The United States has supply and communications bases in Salvador, which are used by the Contras operating in Nicaragua.

— Honduras has had no dialogue with the guerilla movements operating in its jurisdiction, and has been condemned since Esquipulas by the Inter-American Court of Human Rights for violations of human rights. Its amnesty decree has been taken advantage of by about forty people. It is permanently occupied by American troops and houses Contra bases and encampments.

— Costa Rica maintains that most of the provisions of the accord do not apply to it since there are no deep divisions within Costa Rican society. They say dialogue takes place in the Legislative Assembly, and there is complete freedom of speech and assembly there. However it remains an important propaganda base for the Contras, and they operate radio stations from there.

These rather uneven developments in the various countries of Central America show how slow a regional process for peace and democracy can be. However, it is on Nicaragua that the focus of international attention has been placed. It is the country with most to gain from the plan, because it is now provided with a pan-nationalist framework, and with UN involvement, to demonstrate the development of its democracy and to prove to the world its openness to scrutiny. Such examination will render the US involvement in undermining the Nicaraguan government obsolete. That is the hope. So what has Nicaragua done to implement the spirit of the Peace Plan, and how has the International Commission on Verification judged its progress?

A National Reconciliation Commission was established on 1 September, 1987, and met over twenty times in its first year. Its membership includes Cardinal Miguel Obando Y Bravo (who is President of the Commission), members of the main opposition parties (both those who took part in the 1984 elections and those who refused to participate), the President of the Ecumenical Committee for Development (CEPAD) Dr. Gustavo Parajon, and Dr. Gonzalo Ramirez, President of the Nicaraguan Red Cross. The Commission delivered the most important breakthrough in any country in the region by establishing ceasefire talks, culminating in the Sapoa accord of March 1988. The ceasefire lasted for four months, after which the Contra troops went on the offensive again. It is generally considered, though, that with the fall-off in military aid from the United States they have been less capable of carrying out military operations and are no longer the lynch-pin of the strategy to change the government of Nicaragua. However, they are still capable of inflicting civilian casualties, and already in 1989 they have attacked a northern village, killing six people, and a civilian boat, killing two and injuring seventeen. The Contras have become an increasingly divided and demoralised force, and there is little doubt that a complete cut in funding to them from abroad would lead to a permanent ceasefire. The National Reconciliation Commission could be made responsible for real humanitarian aid to resettle those of them who wish to live in Nicaragua, along with all of those displaced and impoverished by the war of the last eight years.

On the question of amnesty, the Nicaraguan government had already granted an amnesty in 1983 to all prisoners wishing to be reintegrated into civilian life. This has been systematically renewed since 1983, and altogether about 6,000 prisoners have been released under its terms. The government has placed a proposal on the table to free almost all ex-National Guard and Contra prisoners, subject to a definitive ceasefire.

The Commission on Verification of the operation of the Peace Plan speaks supportively of the work of the National Reconciliation Commission in Nicaragua. In their report of the 14 January 1988, they say: 'the purpose of the regional commissions is to promote and support the cease-fire process, ensure effective participation in implementation of the amnesty law, assist the return home of displaced persons, and make it easier for the National Reconciliation Commission to check on the measures adopted by the government with reference to the amnesty of 1985 and a ceasefire' (p. 27). They also noted and welcome the re-opening of the daily newspaper *La Prensa,* and the raising of the censorship of communication media, allowing the resumption of broadcasting by Radio Catolica. They went on: 'The CIVS received information during its visit to Managua that there existed greater scope in Nicaragua for enjoyment of the freedoms of expression and association since the signing of the Guatemala procedure. Despite the persistence of the state of emergency, the government had permitted the holding of meetings without restriction in closed premises, while it had routinely authorised public demonstrations, with a few exceptions.' While this widening of democratic freedoms is to be welcomed, it should be noted that the international commission, under this heading of human rights, speaks of how in El Salvador, 'there were still frequent cases of disappearance, murder, illegal detention, extrajudicial statements obtained under torture and other abuses.' And in Guatemala, the 'National Reconciliation Commission has pointed to persistent complaints by various social groups, particularly trade unionists and politicians, to the effect that human rights continue to be violated in Guatemala. The press often relates cases of missing and murdered persons, crimes that some sectors blame on the government, which in turn attributes them to uncontrolled political forces of the far left and far right'. While Nicaragua has made mistakes in restricting press freedom in the past, it is interesting that the international commission found no one to claim that the most basic rights, to life and bodily integrity, were under threat from the Nicaraguan government. The opposition's main concerns were in the constitutional area, for example, demanding that the army be expressly separated from the Sandinista government in order to preserve its integrity as a national rather than a party army. In other Central American countries such debates might seem like the icing on the cake of democratic freedoms.

Nicaragua has been prepared to look critically at its own performance in the context of the Guatemala agreement, and to move towards the guidelines laid down in the accord. Having lived there, I can see why. There is a desperate need to find any way to stop the Contra war and its support. Only when that happens can the real work of transforming the social and economic structure of Nicaragua begin. They have emphasised the part of the plan which calls for an end to aid to irregular forces by outside governments, and for the countries of Central America not to allow themselves to be used as bases for troops opposing the sovereign governments of the region. In this regard, Nicaragua was glad to note the views of the international commission of verification; 'Despite the exhortation of the Central American presidents, the government of the United States of America persists in its policy and practice of providing assistance, particularly military assistance, to the irregular forces operating against the Government of Nicaragua. Definitive cessation of such assistance continues to be a prerequisite for the success of the peace efforts and of the Guatemalan Procedure as a whole.'

The Esquipulas agreement states: 'The five states will ask the governments of the region and those outside the region that give overtly or covertly military, logistical, financial or propaganda aid, or weapons, personnel ammunition and equipment to irregular forces or insurrectional movements, to cease this aid. This is essential to the achievement of a firm and lasting peace in the Region'. The hope that this view would be supported by countries outside the region was soon dashed as the single-minded determination of the Reagan administration to oust the Nicaraguan government continued to make itself felt. In the year following the accord these were some indicators:

| | |
|---|---|
| August 1987: | President Reagan met the Contra leadership in Washington and announced his intention to continue financing them. |
| September: | A fifty-member congressional delegation arrived in Central America to promote a new 310 million dollar aid package for the Contra war. |
| | The House of Representatives approved 3.5 million dollars in 'humanitarian aid'. |
| November: | 15,500 US soldiers arrived in Honduras. |
| | The *Miami Herald* published a report saying that since the signing of the Esquipulas Accords the US has doubled the flow of military supplies to the Contras and flown forty aerial supply missions to Nicaragua. |
| December: | Congress approved another 17.3 million dollars in 'humanitarian aid'. |
| January 1988: | Elliott Abrams announced an 'unprecedented campaign' for Contra aid, and President Reagan asked congress for 36 million dollars for them. |
| March: | 3,200 soldiers of the US 82nd Airborne division and the 7th Infantry division arrived in Honduras. |
| | Honduran planes bombed Nicaraguan border towns and posts, alleging Nicaraguan army incursions into their territory. |
| April: | Congress approved 17.7 million dollars in 'humanitarian aid'. US air force planes arrived in Honduras with supplies from the Agency for International Development. |
| August: | Secretary of State George Schultz arrived in Central America, and tried to get the regional foreign ministers to sign a document which was strongly antagonistic to Nicaragua. They refused. |
| | The Senate approved 27 million dollars in |

'humanitarian aid' and the release of another 16 million dollars, frozen until then.

The United States does not appear to have been moved in the period following Esquipulas to scale down its intervention against Nicaragua. In fact the Assistant Secretary of State for Inter American Affairs said in November of 1987 that the US 'is not prepared to cede to the commission (i.e the Commission of Verification on Esquipulas) the right to decide its policy in Central America.' The accession of George Bush to the White House may herald a change in US policy on Contra funding. There is no doubt that he does not have the messianic commitment to the Contras that President Reagan had. Nevertheless, he was part of the Reagan administration, and involved in the Iran-Contra arms shipment. If there is to be a real change and development in US policy with regard to Nicaragua it will come from pressure from the US Congress, from international opinion, and from the developing dialogue among the Central American presidents themselves.

Since I left Nicaragua, journalistic reports and those of friends returning from there indicate that the economic situation has deteriorated a great deal since 1987. Most of all, the purchasing power of the poor has declined to the point where real hunger is commonplace. In February 1988, the government tried to alleviate this situation by pegging the US dollar at a fixed low rate to the cordoba. While this increased the spending power of the working-class, it caused a drying-up of much-needed dollars in the Nicaraguan economy. A further set of economic measures was introduced in June, and this index-linked the dollar to inflation.

Inflation is running at several thousand per cent. The reason is the scarcity of goods, and the spiralling of paper money to meet the few commodities available. Nearly a quarter million people are employed in the non-productive state sector, in the army, police and Ministry of the Interior. The government is attempting to involve the army in productive agricultural work, but this can only become a reality if the military threat decreases, freeing soldiers to tend crops. In the meantime, a free market is allowed to exist, and with demand in excess of supply, prices continue to rocket.

In an interview for 'Radharc' on RTE television last year, Xavier Gorostiaga evaluated Nicaragua's deep economic crisis: '60% of it is due to the war; 10% to the collapse of the Central American Common Market; 10% to the international crisis and the deteriorating terms of trade for Nicaragua's produce, and there are two internal costs: 10% is caused by lack of investment by the private sector, and 10% by the failures and errors of the Sandinista government. But basically, the cause of the economic crisis is the war of aggression organised, led and financed by the United States government.'

Kate Hughes, my Scottish friend, is just home from Nicaragua. She says that it's hard to imagine that people can survive the economic situation much longer without some let-up. The work is so hard and so long, merely to survive. People are beginning work at five in the morning, getting things ready to sell, travelling for miles to markets or the city, and working all day into the late evening. Poverty is driving people to crime, and robberies, even armed robberies, have become quite commonplace. The government has tried various economic strategies, but the squeeze on loans and finance and the drain of the war have made ordinary people's lives even harder than before.

With all of the economic difficulties it already has, it is barely believeable that Nicaragua has had to deal with another major natural disaster. In October 1988, Hurricane Joan wended its destructive way across the Caribbean, skirting the coast of Colombia, threatening the island of San Andres. The Sandinista Government moved in anticipation of the disaster. 324,000 people, or one twelfth of the population, were evacuated from the expected path of the hurricane. This evacuation led to minimal loss of life in such a huge storm.

The Atlantic coast was hit hardest. On the Corn Islands, 70 kilometres out in the Caribbean, barely a tree let alone a house was left standing.[1] Bluefields, the coast's biggest city, was almost completely destroyed, and its population of

38,000 left virtually homeless. The central river town of Rama was completely flooded as the river Escondido burst its banks and the water rose by 16 metres. As well as the destruction of homes and towns, agriculture was badly hit, with torrential rains destroying coffee crops in Matagalpa and Jinotega. Tens of thousands of cattle and pigs were killed by the hurricane and 130,000 chickens destroyed. The estimated cost in agricultural production was 90 million dollars. The cost of infrastructural damage was 718 million dollars[2]. In addition, the ecological effects will only be seen over the next few decades. Ten per cent of the country's total vegetable cover was lost and this may lead to serious climatic changes. The loss of the forest which took so much of the brunt of the disaster will lead to further flooding and even warmer tropical winds in the years to come.

In the end it was a disaster comparable to the earthquakes of 1972. 137 people were killed, 185 injured, 119 missing and 186,000 made homeless. Many more people would have been killed had it not been for the evacuation of the area in advance. Nevertheless, the job of rebuilding towns and houses is a huge one, and is continuing as I write. And the tropical forest, beautiful as well as useful, is gone, replaced by the unrelenting brown of the post-hurricane landscape. It is said to resemble a bombed-out war zone. The Economic Commission on Latin America has tallied the total damages at 840 million dollars, with capital damages exceeding 540 million dollars. 231,000 people, corresponding to 38,588 families, have lost everything that they possessed, and another 78,000 have been indirectly affected.

The response of the economic community to the disaster has been uneven. Cuba sent a team of hurricane experts in advance of the storm's arrival, despite having itself been lashed by Hurricane Gilbert only a month previously. By the Monday after the storm, seven planes arrived from Cuba with relief supplies, and several shipments went directly to the Atlantic coast itself. Promises of support came in very quickly from Sweden, Mexico, the Soviet Union and the European Community. The EC contributed 750,000 very welcome dollars. But the United States, even in the face of this natural disaster, refused to contribute money or goods.

On the 24   of October, just two days after the hurricane hit, the Voice of America radio station called on other countries not to give aid to Nicaragua, saying that the government could not be trusted to give it to the people in need.

The Nicaraguan government has impressed the usually sceptical people of the Atlantic coast with the level of their direct involvement in the post-hurricane work. The president himself, Daniel Ortega, went to Bluefields before Hurricane Joan struck to check on the preparations. Elsewhere, Commandantes Victor Tirado and Carlos Nunez supervised operations in Regions V and VI, while in Managua Tomas Borge led a brigade securing property and persuading residents to go to the shelters provided. The Sandinista trade unions and their youth and women's organisations spearheaded the clean-up and rebuilding programme throughout the country.[3] If the level of the disaster was similar to that of 1972, the response at least seems to have been very different.

In the period following the hurricane, the people of Bluefields themselves got involved in committees and work in an unprecedented fashion. There were brigades for cleaning up the debris, health brigades, food distribution and building brigades. In the first month alone, these brigades succeeded in cleaning most of the streets, preventing any outbreaks of epidemics, returning electricity to 27 blocks, reroofing the hospital and repairing thousands of damaged houses. The work is co-ordinated by the Moravian church, the principal denomination on the Atlantic coast. When asked about the effects of statements broadcast into the area by the Contra radio station in this period, Rene Enriquez, who works with the church's social assistance agency, said he had seen very little negative reaction against the government. In a meeting of nearly one hundred people in his barrio, one man tried to speak against the government but he received no support. Similarly, a campaign by *La Prensa* against a Cuban offer to rebuild one thousand houses seems to have backfired. A Maronite pastor and former mayor of Bluefields, Brother Ray Hodgson, took 3,000 signatures to Managua condemning the *La Prensa* articles. It 'offended our intelligence by trying to make us appear colonised by the Cubans' said a member of the delegation, Ricardo Morales. 'Besides, it's unjust to treat them that way, when there's not a single costeño (person from the Atlantic coast) who's not thankful for that aid.'[4]

This book began with an earthquake in 1972, which even now leaves Managua pockmarked and devastated. It finishes with another tragedy, the hurricane of 1989. In between, Nicaraguan society has profoundly changed, not least in its response to such tragedies. The new optimism is reflected in a moving article written by Sofia Montenegro in *Barricada*, on 29 October, 1988, just a week after the flood. She concludes, 'Our tenacity comes from this almost innate obstinacy to follow the same path as many times as necessary, to come into our own as people, as a nation, fully and authentically, without the chains of poverty, without foreign domination, and less vulnerable in the face of natural disasters. The very effort of trying to make it to the summit is enough to fill one's heart. This gigantic rock that is Nicaragua is nothing without us. And without it, we are nothing as well.'[5]

1. Letter from Chris Taylor, working with Barricada Internacional, November 1988. Available Nicaragua Solidarity Campaign, London.
2. Report given by President Daniel Ortega, to the National Assembly, 15th November 1988.
3. Letter from Chris Taylor, November 1988.
4. *Envio*, 'Blufilenos Gettin' It Together', January 1989.
5. *Envio*, Special Section on Hurricane Ioan, January 1989.

# BIBLIOGRAPHY AND FURTHER READING

Barry, Tom and Preusch, Deb, *The Central American Fact Book*, New York, Grove Press Inc., 1981.

Brody, Reed, *Contras Terror in Nicaragua*, Boston, South End Press, U.S.

Cassidy, Sheila, *Audacity to Believe*, London, Collins, 1978.

*Central America – Options for the Poor*, Oxfam File.

Dickey, Christopher, *With the Contras*, New York, Simon and Schuster, 1985.

Didion, Joan, *El Salvador*, London, The Hogarth Press, 1983.

Dixon, Marlene and Jones, Susanne (eds), *Nicaragua Under Siege*, San Francisco Synthesis Publications, 1984.

Dorr, Donal, *Option for the Poor*, Maryknoll, Orbis Books, 1983.

Keogh, Dermot, *Central America – Human Rights and US Foreign Policy*, Cork University Press, 1985.

Marnham, Patrick, *So Far From God. A Journey to Central America*, London, Jonathan Cape, 1985.

Metcalf, John, *Letters from Nicaragua*, London, CIIR, 1988.

*Nicaragua — the Sandinista Peoples' Revolution* (compilation of articles), New York, Pathfinder Press, 1985.

*Nicaragua – An Unfinished Canvas*, Dublin, Nicaraguan Book Collective, 1988.

O'Brian, Niall, *Revolution from the Heart*, Dublin, Veritas, 1985.

Pearce, Jenny, *Under the Eagle, US Intervention in Central America and the Caribbean*, London, Latin American Bureau, 1981.

Rushdie, Salman, *The Jaguar Smile*, London, Picador, 1987.

Tijerino, Doris, *Inside the Nicaraguan Revolution*, as told to Margaret Randall, Vancouver, New Star Books, 1978.

Weber, Henri, *Nicaragua, The Sandinist Revolution*, Verso, London, 1981.